PALEO
Meal Planning
on a Budget

PALEO
Meal Planning
on a Budget

Elizabeth McGaw

Front Table Books • An Imprint of Cedar Fort, Inc.

Springville, Utah

ISBN: 978-1-4621-1506-8

Published by Front Table Books, an imprint of Cedar Fort, Inc.
2373 W. 700 S., Springville, UT, 84663
Distributed by Cedar Fort, Inc., www.cedarfort.com

Library of Congress Cataloging-in-Publication data on file

Cover and page design by Bekah Claussen
Cover design © 2014 by Lyle Mortimer
Edited by Rachel Munk

Printed in the United States of America

10 9 8 7 6 5 4 3 2 1

Contents

Meal Planning

Recipes

Breakfast

Lunch

Dinner + Side Dishes

Desserts + Snacks

Quick Reference

Meal Planning

Introduction

There are a lot of things I could start off this book by telling you—such as why I'm Paleo, how short and hyper I am, or that I have a really cute dog—but what I really want to tell you is why I'm so passionate about meal planning. Let me preface by saying that I know this book is titled *Paleo Meal Planning on a Budget*, but honestly, you don't have to be Paleo to read this book. You could eat a regular American diet, or you could be into the whole carb-loading-with-tons-of-pasta-diet—is that even still a diet? What matters is that you're on a budget and you want to learn how to meal plan, or maybe you just plain *need* to learn to meal plan. By the end of this book, you're going to know all of your options when it comes to meal planning, and you'll also get to drool over some really yummy food pictures.{Have you flipped to the back of the book yet? No? I'll wait—go look!}

Why is meal planning so important? Simply because it's the best and most effective way to keep you and me on our budgets every week. Meal planning allows you to say, "I have *x* dollars to spend this week, and I'm going to do it by eating *a*, *b*, and *c*. It will also allow you to allocate money for stocking up on food and other items for when you've got some really slim weeks budget-wise—so you'll still have plenty to eat without having to compromise! Sounds pretty awesome, right? Well, it is. I would never have gotten through the last four-plus years being Paleo without one kind of meal planning or another. And by no means am I asking you to make elaborate meal plans with prep strategies every week. Sometimes it's enough if you just make a mental list of what you want to eat for the week. I've done that before, and while it's not as effective for me personally, it still works. If, however, you're super busy and have a family or you feed more than just yourself, a well-planned meal plan with a prep strategy will keep you on schedule and make your life a little bit easier!

And now that you know why I'm so in love with meal planning, let me introduce myself! Hi! I'm Liz. I'm short, hyper, I have a really cute dog and a disgruntled cat, and I like really long walks on the beach while drinking coffee. Okay, maybe not the long walks on the beach part {I prefer to be lazy on the beach}, but definitely the drinking coffee part. I run a really epic blog called *Paleo on a Budget*, where all the cool kids hang out. I talk about all things Paleo and budget-related, and also, you know, about other hilarious or random things that might not have anything to do with Paleo or budgets.

I've been Paleo for four-plus years and I LOVE to cook. I've been cooking since I was a kid, and we can all thank my dad for my passion and love for it. I can also thank him for my ability to properly julienne an onion without slicing a finger off—thanks, Dad! And then there's Paleo. Oh Paleo, how I love you and what you've done for me. Not only has Paleo given me back my energy, it's also helped me cure all my stomach problems, drop all my excess weight, and let me sleep well at night. And it's allowed me to be happy. You read that one, right? I'm happy! Which, when you've spent your teenage and young adult years being overweight and miserable, is a huge deal.

Fun fact: *Paleo on a Budget* is such a cool kid concept and awesome blog, that last year I wrote this really amazing book called *Paleo on a Budget: Saving Money, Eating Healthy*. It's a cookbook full of yummy, easy, budget-friendly recipes, along with an overview on the ins and outs of being on a tight budget. I even have some information on how to blend a Paleo and Non-Paleo household! So, after reading this book, if you need more recipes to build even more epic meal plans, check out my first book!

So now that you know all about me, let me tell you all about this pretty cool thing called Paleo.

Paleo 101

Paleo is a way of eating based on the foods your great—times way too many zillion—great-grandparents ate as the original hunter-gatherers. They ate a diet mainly of lean meat, fish, vegetables, fruits, and assorted nuts and seeds. This means that their diet was full of good fats and lots of protein, and—when you think about it—it's probably what you want in your daily diet if you have to, let's say, hunt wild animals with spears and no protective gear. It wasn't until many, many, many years later that the agricultural revolution hit and humans started to eat grain-based foods. Fast forward a few—okay, more than a few—hundred years to 1975, when our friend Dr. Walter L. Voegtlin wrote *The Stone Age Diet*. This was arguably the first formal, modern write-up of the Paleo diet/movement. I'm calling it modern because if you look throughout history, you'll see patches of time where people were encouraged to eat things like healthy fats and proteins and to slow their roll on bad carbohydrates, all of which are huge components of being Paleo. If you want more information on the modern history of what people were encouraged to eat and why fats and proteins are good for you, check out the Gary Taubes and his books *Good Calorie, Bad Calorie* and *Why We Get Fat*. Both are excellent resources and make the nerd in me happier than a kid at Christmas!

I'm pretty happy and excited that, with Paleo, you're going to get the same benefits of eating a high fat and high protein diet like your ancestors did, without the whole hunting-a-wild-animal-with-a-spear part {unless you're into that, which is totally cool}. The Paleo Diet allows you to get back to basics and find out what your body does and does not want to use as fuel, all while making you look extra pretty and giving you a ton more energy than you started with.

Here's a generalized list of what you should and shouldn't eat when rocking the Paleo way of life.

Meat, poultry, eggs, fish, vegetables, fruits, healthy oils {olive oil, coconut oil, and so on}, nuts, and some seeds.

Grains, legumes, soy, corn, artificial sugars/sweeteners, processed oils {such as canola and vegetable oil}, gluten, overly-processed foods, and wheat.

Dairy, white rice, raw honey, maple syrup, chocolate, Paleo sweets, and white potatoes.

If you're a long-time Paleo or have done your homework already, you're going to look at my lists and think, "Liz, why are raw honey and maple syrup on the 'maybe' list?" Good question! It's mainly because whether you should or shouldn't eat these foods will depend on your goals for your body. If you're looking to lose weight, then eating lots of raw honey, Paleo sweets, and maple syrup might not be the best idea! If, however, you're looking to maintain your weight, work out super intensely, or want bulk up a bit, adding in those items won't hurt you—unless you have an allergy to one of those foods, of course.

So now that you have your list of foods ready and you know a few of the basic facts, are you feeling good about everything? Great! But wait—you just Googled Paleo again, didn't you? And you've found a bunch of articles saying "don't eat this" and "do eat that" and "eat organic and grass-fed only" or "this year everyone's into doing _____ to stay even healthier!" Can we just talk about confusing and overwhelming? I know, I know, I'm right there with you. So what do you do? You do what feels right for you, your body, and your wallet! Seriously, it's just that simple. Personally? I think there are two things that you should strive for when being Paleo or, in fact, just eating and living in general.

Numero Uno: Only eat what you can afford. If you can't afford organic, pasture-raised or grass-fed, that's okay. I know that for myself, the first year I started Paleo I worried about what I was eating and what I could afford—a lot. It's a totally natural thing to worry about, but I promise it's not necessary. Eating the ground beef and frozen veggies you bought from Walmart instead of from the local organic store is totally fine. It's still going to be a million times better than eating pasta and sauce from a can tonight for dinner. And seriously, if the Paleo Police show up at your door tonight because of the Walmart stuff, just give me a call and I'll totally come bail you out.

Numero Dos: Eat what feels good for you. Paleo is—and should be—really personal. Therefore, what you eat should depend on you, not what someone tells you will work. My favorite yoga instructor, Tara Stiles, encourages people to do what feels good for their individual bodies. She's also a huge fan of mind-set: if it doesn't feel good, don't do it! That's crazy, right? You see where I'm going with this? You need to live in balance with your body and its needs. If you'd rather at times {or all the time} be really strict and follow someone's specific guidelines to the letter, then go for it! But you can also live outside those lines and move around a bit. Try out different foods. See how dairy feels, see how white rice or white potato might feel. You never know what you're going to find out about yourself and your body. Just make sure you're constantly checking in with yourself to see if you're eating all the right foods, and modify as your body changes and as your body goals change!

If you want more information on the different kinds of eating programs for Paleo, or the tech specs of why this is all really good for you and your body, check out a few of these awesome books: {All of these authors also have fantastic blogs and social media pages as well, so make sure to Google them if you haven't before!}

▶ Rob Wolff — *The Paleo Solution*

▶ Melissa and Dallas Hartwig — *It Starts with Food*

▶ Mark Sisson — *The Primal Blueprint*

▶ Diane Sanfilippo — *Practical Paleo*

All right, now that we've made friends with each other and I've given you the know-how on being Paleo, how about we go turn you into a meal-planning machine!

Meal Planning

Many times, you might approach meal planning the same way you pin on Pinterest {you know exactly what I'm talking about}. When you pin on Pinterest, you think something is a really cool idea, but then you think, "I'll probably never do it or buy it or try it." The same thing goes for meal planning: "Eh, it's really a cool idea, but I'll probably just never do it."

Well, that stops here as of right now {or whenever you finish this book, whichever comes first}. And then, after you get this whole meal planning thing under your belt, we'll talk more about your Pinterest boards and see what we can check off those lists.

So let's talk to about the basics, shall we? Meal planning is really, really simple, but there are many options and variations that you can follow. Which is why if you've already skimmed through this book, you'll notice that I broke meal planning down into as many pieces as I could—oh yeah, I went super geeky, nerdy, hyper Liz on you—to ensure that you know all of the options available to you. I also did it so you can troubleshoot when something isn't working for you! However, in order to be successful at it, all you need to know is what you're in the mood to eat this week, what's on sale at your grocery store, and how much time you have to cook and prepare everything.

Simple enough, right? See, I told you! And if you've fast forwarded already to other sections in this book, you've seen that there is a multitude of different ways for you to accomplish it! This means that how you meal plan is flexible, and can change and adapt with you from week to week, depending on what your schedule is. It's awesome!

But the bigger—or dare I say biggest—question is: why meal plan? I honestly think that there are probably a million and one different reasons to meal plan {that could be a tad bit dramatic, but you get the idea}. The main and most important reason is simple: meal planning will allow you to maximize your weekly grocery budget all the time. You'll never wonder how you're going to pay for dinner or lunches this week, because it'll be well-planned out and you'll have a rough idea of how much you're spending. It will absolutely help you get through those weeks when you don't have two pennies to rub together, and it'll keep you from overspending when you find yourself with a few extra dollars in your pocket.

As a bonus, meal planning also makes your life easier when it comes to cooking. If you know what you're cooking for the week and when you want to eat it, you can start to develop a strategy to prepping some small things ahead of time. Which means you'll spend less time in the kitchen and more time being awesome, doing whatever it is you'd rather be doing!

Figuring Out Your Budget

If you're anything like me, this section is going to be exciting in a geeky, I-get-to-use-the-calculator-on-my-phone sort of way. If not, I'm really sorry, but don't leave! You need to know this information!

Everyone still here? Good, let's get started!

Knowing your budget and how to figure it out is probably the most important thing you can take away from this book. Knowing what you have to spend, what you need to spend, and what your financial goals are is crucial to doing anything on a budget.

Let's start with knowing how much you make a month. Add in any income you bring in that can be put toward bills, living expenses, and so on. Got it? Good!

Now write out a list of all your bills, and I'm talking everything: car payments, car insurance, rent/mortgage, homeowners insurance, Netflix, gas, electric, cable, Internet, cell phones, pet care, your kids' sports and school activities, credit card debt, and so on. And if you're self-employed or make any kind of income that you yourself will have to pay taxes on, don't forget to include your quarterly or monthly tax deductions! You can also include any money that you would like to put away for something specific {such as a down payment on a house, braces for your kids, a trip to the Paleo FX next year, a rainy day fund, and so on}.

Now add it all up and breathe, because that number isn't as scary as it seems to be, I promise! Subtract your monthly income from your monthly expenses. That's what you have for the month to spend on things like food, household essentials, and anything fun you want to do {like going to the movies or visiting a museum}. How's your breathing? You doing okay so far?

Now that you know that end number, you can figure out how much of it you want to put toward your grocery bill and how much you want to put toward other things. That number all comes down to a personal preference; if eating organic, grass-fed, expensive-ish foods is super important to you, then you'll be putting more into your food budget. If you'd rather go out on the town or see a movie once a week, then that's where most of your money will go. You can also go monkey-in-the-middle and put half toward one and half toward the other. If that number is already small, you're going to have to do what I did, which is cut out the fun extra-curricular activities and put the extra money toward your grocery/household items.

How's that number looking to you? Is it a little too lean, or are you surprised you have that much money to spend? For most of us that number is going to be well beyond too lean. You might need a few ideas on how to save money outside of just cutting back on what you spend for groceries or other activities! On the next page you'll find a brief list of some things you can skim back on to save a few extra dollars. These are all things I've done over the course of being Paleo in order to save money, and to also have more money for the kind of lifestyle I want to have {which is mainly being my own boss, working to be debt-free, and eating really healthy}. This list is by no means your only option when it comes to saving money. I'm sure other options are available to you. A great way to figure out what they are is to look at your finances and see if there's any wiggle room in those items!

In the meantime, here's my list to get you started on saving a few extra dollars every month:

▶ Cancel the cable: Cable is ridiculously expensive! You can save anywhere from twenty to one hundred dollars a month by cutting out the cable and just keeping the Internet {or Internet and home phone}. And sports fans—don't grumble at me! If you don't want to miss out on your favorite sporting events, I'd suggest looking into an online subscription! You can get the MLB network, for instance, and have access to tons of games! But before you go that route, make sure you check out their black-out restrictions to make sure you'd still be able to see some of the games you want to. Or maybe you're a TV show/movie buff: look into an Amazon Prime or Netflix Subscription! I'm finding that both options are updated with full seasons of my favorite shows more and more often—and as a bonus, if you sign up for Amazon Prime you can get free two-day shipping on most purchases! If you want to watch current shows right when they come out, check out a subscription to Hulu! Or heck, check out that particular show's station online, because sometimes you'll find that they post recent episodes! All three options {Netflix, Amazon Instant Prime, and Hulu} have free trials, so if you're not sure if you can live without cable, you can test it out first!

▶ Check out your cell phone bill: How expensive is your cell phone bill right now? Are you actually getting a good deal, or are you getting a good deal for what they offered you? For instance, have you signed up for 6 GB of data for your smart phone when you're only using 2 GB per a month? Or maybe you have unlimited text messaging, but you really only send an average of two hundred a month. Most of the time by reevaluating your cell phone bill, you can save anywhere from ten to thirty dollars a month!

▶ Car + Home/Renters Insurance: A lot of times once we sign up for a company, we stay with them for years and years and are really good customers! You can always try calling them up and seeing if they're running any promotions or if they offer any kinds of discounts for loyal customers. A lot of times those deals aren't advertised, but you could receive them simply by calling up! This can apply to almost any non-utility company that you've been with for a long time.

▶ Be aware of the basics: This tip might sound lame or old school, but it's considered tried and true for a reason! Be familiar with your day-to-day activities and utility usage in your home. Electricity and gas are expensive, so make sure you're turning off the lights when you leave a room and that you're not leaving the TV on if you're not watching it. When it's the holiday season, don't leave your lights on outside for the whole night; just pick a few hours to have them on. It won't save you a ton of money, but it will add up over time!

▶ Combine trips when running errands: When you need to run errands, double check that you actually need those items right then and that you don't just want to get them so you can get out of the house. And if you do need said items, can you combine this trip with any other errands? Cutting down your number of trips to the store will not only save you on gas for your car, but also on its maintenance! And if you do want to get out to just to get out, then go for a walk. Take whoever is home with you and go explore the surrounding areas—you never know what crazy fun you can get up to!

▶ Creative-ish options for fun activities: Let's say you love hanging out with your friends but you really don't have the budget to go out with them all the time or even to pay to have them all over—that's totally fine! Just get creative. Invite them all over and ask everyone to bring an appetizer, and do a finger food kind of party. Or ask everyone to bring a dish to dinner—it's okay to ask for help when you need it! Or maybe you really want to see the newest superhero movie, but it's way out of your budget to see it at the theater. Just give it a few months and it'll be at something like a Redbox where you can rent it for really cheap {I'm talking like a quarter of the price of your movie ticket}! And the bonus is: you can watch the movie with as many people as you want from the comfort of your own couch with your own snacks.

Those are just a few ways to save a few extra dollars when money gets tight. You don't have to implement them all—heck, you don't have to do any of them. Just know these options are available to you in case things start to get really, really tight.

Before You Meal Plan

Before you start meal planning like a pro, there's one thing you might want to do: create yourself a pantry and stash of stock-up items. Now I'm not asking you to go couponing crazy on me and have five hundred rolls of toilet paper and paper towels on hand at all times—I don't even know where you'd put that much toilet paper! What I am asking you to do is keep the basics on hand as often as possible. This will allow you to create any meal, planned or last minute, without having to stress about it.

You can just stick with the bare essentials and have herbs, spices, and canned goods in your pantry, or you can take it to the next level and start stocking up on things like meats and frozen vegetables. You can even have different stocks, soups, and other quick pre-made dinners on hand if you want! My favorite part? By keeping stocked up on these items, you can buy these items in the future only when they're at a good price, which means you're never going to have to overpay for them!

There's a really good reason I'm so adamant about this, but it's going to involve a super quick story! Ready?

When I first went Paleo, Mr. POAB and I were dirt poor. I'm talking both self-employed with no-idea-where-our-next-pay check-was-coming-from poor. When we'd find ourselves doing okay money-wise, I'd make sure to buy extra things like ground meat and frozen vegetables if they were on sale. At the time it almost seemed excessive, but I figured what was the harm, it was all on sale and we'd eat it at some point. Then fast forward a few weeks later, and once again we find ourselves literally counting our pennies to see if we could make it to the next client payment. Which, in reality, meant that we had no money for groceries. I ended up only buying two dozen eggs, onions, and some butter that week, and we lived on stir frys, eggs, and whatever else you can make from that combination for almost two weeks. If we hadn't had that supply of extra meat and vegetables, I have no idea how we would have been able to afford food and our bills that month. Which is the main reason I push for this all the time: you never know when you're going to need every single penny you have to spend on things other than groceries or household items.

You could be a little overwhelmed right now, just thinking of all the things you need to suddenly go out and buy—which is totally normal—but don't be! This isn't something you need to have magically appear over night in your cabinets and freezer. You can take your time and stock up little by little, until you have everything you want to have on hand! Personally, it took me the better part of three months to have a nice little stash of what I wanted, while using what I had when I needed it. So take it slow and stock up when you have the extra money and when things are on sale!

Need a little inspiration on what to stock up on? On the next page is a list of my favorite items to have on hand. If you see an item with a * next to it, it means that you can find coupons or store deals for these items on a fairly regular basis, so don't settle for full price on them! Also, some of these items aren't food—some might say they're not even Paleo—but things like aluminum foil, trash bags, and gallon-size freezer bags have made my life so much easier, so I included them on the list!

For the Cabinets

▶ Favorite dried herbs:

   Mine are oregano, basil, parsley, italian seasoning, rosemary, thyme, and dill.

▶ Favorite spices:

   Mine are cumin, chili powder, garlic powder, cinnamon, and red hot pepper flakes.

▶ Vanilla extract {good quality}

▶ Nut flours, generally coconut and almond flour* {I actually store the unopened ones in the freezer because it makes them last longer!}

▶ Canned diced tomatoes

▶ Canned crushed tomatoes

▶ Aluminum foil*

▶ Gallon-size freezer bags*

▶ Plastic wrap*

▶ Sandwich bags*

▶ Paper towels*

▶ Coconut oil*

▶ Olive oil*

▶ Extra-light olive oil*

▶ Enjoy Life chocolate chips {They're dairy, nut, and soy free!}

▶ Coffee and assorted teas

For the Freezer and Fridge

▶ Favorite cuts of steak

▶ Cube steak

▶ Boneless skinless chicken breast

▶ Chicken thighs*

▶ Frozen mixed vegetables {I prefer steamfresh bags}*

▶ Frozen broccoli*

▶ Frozen green beans*

▶ Frozen kale

▶ Frozen spinach

▶ Frozen sausages {my favorite brand is Applegate}

▶ Bacon {lots of bacon!}

▶ Pork of some kind, generally pork loin or boneless pork chops

▶ Butter

Other Random Items

I like to keep hot sauce and mustard on hand {in large quantities} because they're two of my favorite condiments! I also like to stock up in early winter {the start of the cold and flu season} on tissues because they generally go on sale at this time and you can find online coupons for them. I buy them all once at a ridiculously good price and have them for most of the year!

From this list of semi-basic goodies, you can literally make a dozen different meals, all of which can be turned into leftovers or used to create an entirely new meal! So go check out that store circular and start stocking up!

How to Meal Plan

I think the hardest part of meal planning is knowing where to start. Do you create a meal plan and then create a grocery list for it, or do you create your meal plan based on what's on sale at your store this week? And when should you create your meal plan and prep for it? How far in advance should you actually create the meal plan itself? A week, two weeks, a month? And should your meals consist of all meals that do double duty, or should you have some nights that are just a one-time meal? The list of questions can go and on.

The most important thing to remember is that the answer to all of these questions is "yes." I know, that's confusing, but go with me for a minute. You can literally build your meal plan with whatever foundation makes the most sense to you. If you want to eat whatever is on sale this week, then build your meal plan off your favorite grocery store circular. If you want to eat what's in your freezer, then build your plan off that. If you stock up often enough or have a good idea of what's going to be on sale at your grocery store for the next few weeks, you can absolutely plan your meals up to a month in advance! Personally? I love to build my plans with a mix of what I have on hand in my fridge/freezer and what's on sale at my store. And I normally only plan a week in advance, but I always have a list in the back of my mind of what I can start doing this week to make next week even easier.

Now it's about to get really crazy: I'm going to take you through the different basic options you have on how to meal plan. Keep in mind that these are just a few of the more common options. You can mix and match, or create your own method—this is just to give you a starting point.

#1 Already Have It: Creating a meal plan and then shopping for it.

This kind of meal planning is better for people who stock up a lot and always have a freezer full of meats and vegetables. The shopping part is usually for your normal, everyday stuff like eggs, onions, sweet potatoes, and so on, mixed with mainly stock-up shopping. The beauty of this kind of meal planning is that it doesn't matter what's on sale at the store this week! You've already got 95 percent of it at home, so it's pretty budget friendly, because you purchased all the big stuff at a ridiculously good price! If you're someone who stocks up a ton but likes to meal plan differently, I'd suggest that you do this kind of meal planning at least once every few months to make sure you're using everything you've bought. There's nothing worse than buying certain foods and then finding out that they ended up getting gross in the freezer!

#2 Checking Out the Sales: Meal plan based on local sales.

This kind of meal planning is just as fun as option one, and is perfect for people who don't want to have to stock up on a ton of stuff on a regular basis, or for those who don't have the space to stock up regularly. Just take a glance at what's on sale in your store's circular and build your meal plan around it. So if pork loin is on sale this week, you could plan to use that for one or two different dinners that week, and then use leftovers for lunch! I'd still highly suggest stocking up when you can with this type of meal planning, especially on basic meats like ground meat and chicken breast. Those are two of the things you'll use the most often, and you don't want to pay full price for them if you don't have to! And just like with option one, if you do stock up, make sure once every few months you plan your meals heavily around what's in your freezer.

#3 Mixing and Matching: Mixing options 1 and 2

This is my all-time favorite way to meal plan. It allows me to mix and match, depending on my week and what I need. When my schedule is too busy to allow for a grocery trip, I've got what I need on hand, or if I want to head to the store, I can. And I never have to worry about what's on sale at my store. If the sales are terrible this week, I know I'm still set on what to eat for the week. And if the sales are amazing, I always have the option to buy extra to stock up! This is what I'd suggest trying first, as it can also help you decide what makes you the happiest and most efficient when it comes to meal planning. And just like with options one and two, every few months I try to base my meal plan off of what I have on hand to ensure that nothing goes bad!

To figure out exactly what to eat when, it's up to you and how you like to plan. The easiest way is to start with your main meal, which for most of us is dinner. The option you pick will help determine what you have available to eat. Let's say you have ground meat, pork chops, and chicken breast available to you this week on your budget. Start to plan these items out as dinners. It could look something like this:

Night 1	Spaghetti Squash + Sauce
Night 2	Rosemary Pork Chops
Night 3	Lemon Lime Chicken {plan to make a little extra}

Three nights out of seven—not too shabby! Now let's apply the leftovers and another package or two of ground meat for some of these meals to fill out the rest of our week.

Night 4	Vegetable Chili: Use the leftover sauce from Night 1 for your chili base
Night 5	Blueberry Chicken Salad: Use some of the leftover Lemon Lime Chicken
Night 6	Inside-Out Burgers
Night 7	Basic Stir-Fry

Easy as can be, right? From this point you can start pulling leftovers from each of these dinners for breakfast or lunch that week. The leftover Spaghetti Squash can make one lunch, the leftover Lemon Lime Chicken can make Chicken Lettuce Wraps, and the Inside-Out Burgers can make a Burrito Bowl. Then you can just have some leftover Rosemary Chicken for lunch, and some Vegetable Chili for breakfast. Then just fill in the empty slots with breakfast or lunch items as needed, depending on what you either have on hand or what is on sale. Boom! An entire week is planned that quickly!

And don't be afraid to move things around as you plan. To be totally honest with you, I had started with the Vegetable Chili in night one, but it just didn't make sense there because I couldn't utilize the leftovers. So I put the Spaghetti Squash + Sauce there instead, and bumped the Vegetable Chili down a few days in order to utilize the sauce leftovers.

Now let's go over what I think is the trickiest part of meal planning on a budget: making sure you don't meal plan outside of your budget.

So how do you make sure your nomz this week aren't putting you in the poor house? Pre-pricing things out, my friends {which means yes, we're getting nerdy again}. Get that calculator out and get ready to crunch some numbers!

To start your list, write out the basics that you need, no matter what you're going to eat this week {eggs, coconut oil, onions, and so on}. You probably buy these items regularly, so you have a rough idea of the prices. Next to each item on your list, write the price. {Remember to round up!} So if a bag of onions is about $2.70, round it up to $3 to give yourself a little wiggle room. What you do after this depends on which meal-planning method you're using.

If you're going with option number one, you're pretty set as it is. Plan out your meals for the week—you can use the method I mentioned above—using what you have on hand and the "basics" list of things you're picking up at the store. If it looks like you'll need a few things outside of the norm and your stock-up list, add them to the list! Then we get nerdy again: add up the price of the items you already have on the list and subtract it from your budget. This gives you the amount you can spend on stock-up items or anything else you might want to snack on. So pull out that pretty store circular and go to town picking out different items that you need or want to have more of. {I like to keep my calculator out and subtract the amount of each item from it to ensure I don't go over budget.} So if you have $15 left to spend and you want to get a pound of beef that's $4, you'd have $11 left to play with! And if you don't think you need a ton of stuff or your store sales are pretty terrible this week, don't spend your money needlessly; instead, just save it and use it next week, or put it toward a bill.

If you're going with options two or three, then it's a smidge bit more involved. You want to pop open your circular first and see what's on sale. Just get a glimpse of everything so you know what you should and shouldn't plan for meals. For instance, if you see that butternut squash is on sale, you might consider getting one or two and making Butternut Squash Soup this week, and using another one for a side dish or a different dinner. Then plan out your meals based off of your preferred way to meal plan! From there you'll want to double check your list of the basic things you need, add in what you need to make your meals this week, and then put the prices next to everything. Make sure you round up your prices. So if meat is on sale for $4.49 a pound, round it up to $5!

Get that oh-so-pretty calculator out and add it up. Sometimes you strike gold the first time and are able to fit everything in your budget, and other times you need to make some adjustments to make your meals fit your budget. If you ended up going over budget, just re-check your circular or what's in your freezer and try to adjust it accordingly. Once you've got your meals where you want them, you can either leave your meal plan as-is, or if you're into option three, you'll want to put any extra money into stocking up on a few items. Subtract your stock-up items from your leftover money to make sure you don't overspend! So if you have $10 left and you want to get yourself a $1 bag of frozen veggies, you'd subtract it from your $10, giving you $9 left to spend.

The good news? After doing this for a while, you'll be able to leave out the calculator part {and speed up the process} because you'll be able to mentally tally up what you're getting and ballpark how much it's going to cost you. However, if you're on an incredibly tight budget, you might benefit from one of my earlier shopping methods, and whip out the calculator at the grocery store. Mr. POAB {Mr. Paleo on a Budget} and I used to literally add up how much we were spending as we went through the store. This ensured that we were buying only what we could afford. It might make your shopping trip a few minutes longer, but it's seriously worth the effort if you have very limited resources.

So there you have it! That, in a nutshell, is the easiest way to figure out your meal plan and to make sure it fits into your budget. It's not too hard, right? I promise I won't say I told you so or anything. You might still have a few questions on the whole process, so head on over to the Meal Planning Tips on page 18 to find your answers.

Coupons and Store Deals

I wouldn't be me if I didn't have an entire mini-section dedicated to coupons and store deals, now would I? But before we dive in, it's story time again—gather 'round!

My Yiayia {my dad's mother} had the biggest coupon collection when I was a kid. I can vividly remember her and her sister sitting at the kitchen table, going through the store circulars and looking through their little accordion folder of coupons, picking out what they were going to use with what sale that week. They were so pro at this that they did this kind of coupon planning for multiple stores every week, and had backup plans for their original plans. Heck, there might have been a second backup plan, knowing those two.

I'm telling you this awesome story so you can see that I come by my love of coupons and saving money very, very honestly. Because of these women I learned the value of waiting for a deal and stocking up on items when I was able to. They both had their own small stock-up piles of canned goods and household and kitchen essentials, which provided some extra food and supplies for not just them but pretty much whoever needed it. Were they crazy couponers? I don't think so; I think they were just incredibly savvy with their money. So let's take a moment and take a page from Yiayia and Aunt Catherine's book and spend a few minutes checking for coupons while putting together our grocery list.

I don't know about you, but I hate buying the Sunday paper and clipping what I need. {Not to mention how I always get little pieces of coupon paper everywhere because I'm such a messy paper cutter.} You ready for the fancy, high-tech solution? Simply Google [store name] coupon match up. You'll pull up a list of a few different websites {like mine!} that provide coupon match ups for your store so you can easily see what items are on sale and if they have a matching coupon. You can then print out the coupons you need from their respective websites! A lot of these websites are so good at what they do that they'll also let you know when something is a ridiculously good price so you can stock up!

And just as a quick, super big, pro tip: the best kind of deal you can get at your grocery store is when you can find a store sale and then match it up with a coupon. A lot of stores will actually pair up their store sales with a coupon being made available. So let's say you find a really pretty coupon for aluminum foil, what do you do with it? Do you use it right away or hold on to it? Correct answer: hold onto that coupon until right before it expires. Most of the time the sale that matches your coupon won't happen until the coupon is pretty close to expiring. This is just to ensure that anyone that doesn't want to wait or doesn't know about store sales will just use the coupon and vice versa. If the item never goes on sale at your store: oh well, the price won't have changed for you if you wait to use it at the very end; you're just making sure that you get the best possible deal!

A Few Extra Couponing Tips

▶ There are two types of basic coupons: store coupons and manufacturer's coupons. Some stores {like Target at the moment} will take both a store coupon and a manufacturer's coupon for the same item. This is basically gold. If you manage to find a sale, and you can use both coupons on that sale, you should proceed to happy dance.

▶ Store loyalty cards are as good as coupons. Some stores are now offering store debit cards that hook up right to your bank account {so it's not a credit card} and allow you to get a percentage off for using it. Other stores have a card you scan that allows you to build up points to either get a gift card or a free item of some kind. Not sure what your store offers? Go to the customer service desk or hop on their website to see what's available!

▶ Catalinas are also coupons. Some grocery stores or regular stores will print you off random coupons with your receipt. You can use these the same way you use a coupon.

▶ There's a difference between a "purchase" and a "transaction." You'll notice that coupons may say "No more than four like coupons per transaction" or "One coupon per purchase." That just means that for every item you buy that corresponds with the coupon, you need one coupon. So if you buy three of the same item, you need three coupons. And most of the time there's a limit. So you can only have four of those coupons in your entire transaction. As for "One coupon per purchase per transaction," this just means that you can use that coupon on one item in your entire transaction {a transaction is everything you're buying in your shopping trip}. It gets fancier and more complicated than that with coupon verbiage, but those two are the most important bits of information!.

▶ Read your store's coupon policy. It's crucial that if you're going to coupon a lot, you read the policies to make sure you go in fully prepared!

Meal Planning Tips

Want some more awesome tips on meal planning? I've totally got you covered!

Tip #1: Leftovers are your best friend. Seriously, there is no way to do this on tight budget, in a short time frame, without them. Leftovers are not only going to save you money, but time as well. It's so much easier to cook up an extra chicken breast with dinner than it is to try cook one in the morning when you're doing a million and one things to get you and your family out the door.

Tip #2: Start to look at your store circulars and plan your meals for next week 2–3 days before you intend to shop and prep, if at all possible! This will save you from having to plan, shop, and prep all in the same day.

Tip #3: Know what a good sale is. It's crucial that you know what is a good sale in your store. For instance, chicken breast is normally $2.99 per pound for me. Sometimes it goes on sale for $2.29 per pound, and that's a decent deal. If I'm desperate, I'll get it at that price. However, my hold-out-for price is $1.99 per pound, because that's the cheapest it gets around here for me. And some {most} of the time the sales will run full price, so-so price, good sale price, so-so price, full price. Knowing how low your must-have items will go plays a huge part in saving the most money.

Tip #4: Don't be afraid to shop manager's specials or markdowns. These are your second-best friend because of how cheap they can get you your food. But because these are the kind of sales you won't know about until you get there, they can raise the question, "What do I do with it?" You have two options: When you get home, you can reevaluate your meal plan and incorporate it that day or the next day, or you can freeze it and use it next week. I prefer the second option for two reasons. The first is I that already did the work to plan out my meals and I don't want to have to redo it. The second is that this just makes next week that much cheaper, and I've already started to plan it—hello awesome sauce!

Tip #5: When you're at the grocery store, make sure to weigh pre-bagged items. I like to buy carrots and onions in a two- or five-pound bag and normally the people who bag it have a rough idea of how much it's going to weigh, but they don't have to get it exact. By weighing things ahead of time, you can sometimes snag yourself a bag over its advertised weight. That one bag of carrots could actually weigh three pounds instead of two, giving you a few extra carrots for the week!

Tip #6: Plan to eat things like muffins early in the week so they stay fresh. If you follow the Big Prep Day Method, you're going to have one day when you're going to make a handful of things in advance. One of those things is muffins, so planning to eat them on Day 1 or Day 2 will ensure maximum yumminess! You can, of course, store leftovers and then eat them a little bit later in the week, but I always like at least one day where they're super fresh!

Tip #7: When planning out Day 6 or 7, you can use the leftovers from those meals to start out the next week. This will help you have less prepping and cooking to do, and will make your life a little bit easier.

Tip #8: Don't meal plan outside of your time budget for the week. If your week is really, really busy, don't plan on making things that take forever to cook, even with prepping ahead of time. Plan for a bunch of fast stir-frys, or recipes that easily do double duty to cut your cooking time in half!

Tip #9: Don't skip the Prep Strategy section of this book. Do. Not. Do. It! Some people think that a prep strategy isn't super important, but I'd highly disagree. It's equally as important as your meal plan! You'll save so much time if you learn even to do some quick, minor prep work! So just head over there now and read it!

Prep Strategy

Intro

The scariest part of meal planning or just cooking for most people is the actual knowing what to cook, and when, part. Think about it, you've got this great meal plan for the week, you're extremely excited to eat all this yummy food, you've gone shopping for it, and now you realize you have to cook it all. For most of us it stops being fun right about now, and starts to look more and more like work. Why? Because when you get home at eight at night—after working for eight hours, taking the kids here and there, and managing to get a workout in—the last thing anyone wants to do is cook. Which means that takeout or some other form of crap is the easiest and most convenient option for dinner instead of a yummy meal.

But guess what? I get it—I've been there; heck, if we're being honest, I still go there some days. So how do I combat the ever present middle-of-the-week "I don't want to cook" syndrome? I prep my meals as I go! I love prepping so much that I cooked and photographed the cookbook portion of this book using a prep strategy, which made my life not only easier, but it made my wallet very, very happy.

Think of a prep strategy as your cooking assistant. It's there to keep you on task and tell you what's next, and it lets you relax more often than not. And, hello, we both know that I love to relax, so this works perfectly for me! The more literal, straightforward definition of a prep strategy is that it's a game plan for your week of cooking {and eating}. It'll outline what you're cooking when, and will help keep you on schedule for the week, which in turn makes your life easier {and yummier}!

The most important thing to remember is that a prep strategy is a great starting point, but it isn't gospel. Just because you've created a meal plan and a prep strategy, that doesn't mean you can't mix it up, swap one dinner for a different dinner, throw a stir-fry in somewhere when you really don't feel like doing much, or {on a day when you're feeling adventurous} decide to cook something really long and complicated.

Different Kinds of Prep Strategies

There are way too many different ways you could decide to prep your meals for the week, and most of the time it'll vary from week to week, depending on what you're making and what your schedule looks like. Right now I'm going to talk about the two strategies that I'm a fan of and that are the most common. Both are fantastic, and one isn't better than the other—it'll just completely depend on your lifestyle, needs, and what you're look-ing to accomplish that week. I like to call the two methods: The Big Prep Day Method {BPD Method} and the As-You-Go Prep Method {AGP Method}.

My personal favorite is the Big Prep Day; it allows you to do a ton of prep work one day a week, giving you room to prep little things throughout the week. This, in turn, makes your life extra easy! I'm going to break down both methods for you so you can see the general idea of both. If you'd like to see a prep strategy in action, head on over to the Meal Plan area and you'll see both methods being used for each week!

▶ *Big Prep Day Method:* He's a big boy, there's no doubt about it. This prep method is detailed to the max. It's best suited for people who have one day a week when they can dedicate a few hours to cooking. During your big prep you'll do things like make chicken stock, pre-chop veggies, and even pre-blend your spices together to make things like Lemon Lime Chicken {page 109} a breeze! You'll also precook a few different items, which should make dinner really, really easy {and yummy}!

Here's how to plan your own Big Day Prep Method:

Look at your meal plan for the week and write out what things you can do in advance. For example: making chicken stock for soup or pre-making soup, chili, or tomato sauce.

Look at what you're eating for breakfast—if you've got scrambled eggs, muffins, or anything like that that you can pre-make, plan to do that on your prep day.

Plan out your snacks if you haven't done so. If you're going to be snacking on hard-boiled eggs or anything that can be pre-made, your big prep day would be the perfect time to make it! This includes tasks like cutting up pepper strips for snacking, making any flavored dips, or even making a salad dressing if you need to.

Write that "Big Prep Day" list out, but don't overwhelm yourself! Just do what you know you can get done within the time frame you have, without getting stressed out.

Look at the rest of your week. What can you do the night before or the day before for each day of the week? For instance, if you're cooking up Lemon Lime Chicken tonight, can you also cook up a few extra chicken breasts to use for chicken salad in two days? If you're using tomato sauce for spaghetti squash, can you reserve some sauce now and use it for your chili base in a few days? Or are you having salad for lunch or dinner tomorrow night? If you have time, pre-chop the lettuce while dinner is cooking tonight to save time!

Make sure everything is doable for you. Each part of the plan needs to easily work for you, or else it'll do the opposite of what it should do—make your life easier.

Don't forget to ask for help! If you have a significant other, roommate, or kids that you also cook for, don't hesitate to drag them into the kitchen to help you prep! It'll make prepping go faster, and it'll probably make it ten times more fun.

▶ *As-You Go Prep Method*: This method isn't a big boy. He's pretty slim actually, but still very, very pretty! This method is best suited for really busy, on-the-go people who can't afford to dedicate a few hours one day a week to cooking and preparing food for the week. It breaks down to a lot of mini-prepping and cooking your meals when and where you have the time.

Here's how to plan your own As-You-Go Prep Method:

Look at your meal plan for the week and see what little things you can prep the day before the week starts. For instance, if you're snacking on hard-boiled eggs this week, you could make those then. Or you could pre-chop a few veggies for different dinners or lunches right now if you have the time. Also, if you're planning on making soup this week, you might want to make your stock on this day to make your life easier.

Look at your week and see what meals you have that can play double duty for a different meal. If you're going to make Inside-Out Burgers {page 90} one night, can you make extra burgers for lunch tomorrow or to add to a stir-fry, tomato sauce, or chili for another day? Can you cook up extra sweet potatoes one day and use them for lunches or for the Sweet Potato Broccoli Mix {page 68} the next day? Figuring this out now will save you time down the road.

I'm going to repeat myself, but it's crucial: make sure everything is doable for you. Make sure each part of your plan works for you and won't stress you out. Don't be afraid to simplify recipes if you need to. For instance, replace a side dish for the night with one that's either easier, or with some kind of leftover from the last few days. It's okay to mix and match meals to meet your needs.

Tips n' Tricks

Tip #1: Make your own mixes. If you're a huge pancake fan, cookie fan, or you like the Zucchini Sticks {page 94}, pre-make a whole bunch of mixes. You can put them in individual bags and store in the fridge or freezer {almond flour keeps for an extra long time in the freezer!}. It's really easy to do and can save you a lot of measuring and dishes next week or the week after when you want to make an extra special breakfast or rock some Maple Bacon Cookies {page 129}.

Tip #2: Pre-Blend Spices: If you're a chili fan or you like one of these recipes or any recipe in particular, premix the spices and store them in your cupboard. You can have a whole "chili mix" ready to go whenever you're in the mood! Here's a double tip: if you're not sure how much to use of your pre-blended spices, make a single serving of the blend and measure how much it is—your Chili Spice Blend might be anywhere from 4–6 tablespoons total. Then write a note on either the bottle or somewhere easily accessible. This will make it even easier to cook any meal.

Tip #3: Pre-Make Scrambled Eggs: Crazy right? You can pre-make scrambled eggs a few days in advance and have them waiting for you in the morning. Talk about a quick breakfast!

Tip #4: If you're on the go 24/7 and don't have time to make chicken stock or roast up a chicken, there's no shame in the pre-buying game. There are a lot of stores that have high-quality, Paleo chickens ready to go, and the same goes for chicken stock. Just make sure you read the ingredients list carefully. Your chicken shouldn't have soy or sugar in it, and neither should your chicken stock. If you're not sure about something, don't hesitate to ask a store employee or check the company's website to see if you can get some more information.

Tip #5: The slow cooker is your friend! You can turn almost any soup, chili, or stock recipe into a slow cooker–friendly meal. If you're not sure how, just Google whatever it is you'd like to do and you can get a general idea of cooking time and temperature.

Tip #6: Whenever possible, make double the amount of sauce or chili you normally need and freeze the extra. That way, one night next week or the week after, you've already got more than half of your dinner ready to go!

Housekeeping Tips for Meal Plans

This is the moment you and I have been waiting for. You've learned to plan, you've learned to shop, you've even learned about different ways to prep, and now you get to see it all come together! In this section of the book I've included four weeks-worth of meal plans! The shopping lists, both kinds of prep strategies, and the recipes for mostly everything are in the next section of the book. Need a minute for a happy dance? And you're back, yes? Good! Before I let you dive in and drool over the meal plans and recipes, here are a few housekeeping notes:

Shopping Lists: The lists just have ingredients and not amounts. This is just because I don't know your family size, what you want a lot of extra of, if you're doubling up on a recipe, and so on. Plus stock-up items might need to be added into to some of these, so just add in how many {or much} you need of each. I'm also including an "other" section in the shopping list with items you probably won't need to buy, like your favorite fat, olive oil, almond flour, and so on. It's just a quick, little, friendly reminder that you'll need it so you can make sure you have enough on hand.

The Meal Plans: Each meal plan will have a page reference next to recipes that require it for easy finding! When it comes to basic things like making mayo, chicken stock, hard-boiled eggs, and so on, check out the Quick Reference Section, beginning on page 138. You'll notice that all the meal plans have Meal 1, Meal 2, and Meal 3. I'm basing the meal plans on the "normal" 3 meals a day, but if you eat more or less than that, you can spread things out accordingly or add in more hard-boiled eggs, fresh vegetables, raw nuts, and such. The days are labeled as Day 1, Day 2, and so on, because everyone's week can start on a different day, depending on scheduling. However, Days 6 and 7 are generally meant to be your two off days of the week, which is why those recipes are a bit more involved.

Feel free to swap days around, swap out breakfast for lunch and vice versa, or change up the side dishes! The meal plans are mainly a starting point for you, so you can then go and customize each week to fit you, your family, and what's on sale this week. And if you already have favorite recipes for some of the dishes in here, you can totally swap mine out for them instead! Just adjust your grocery list and prep strategy accordingly if you need to.

Making Extras: When it comes to things like sauce, chili, and stock, you are more than welcome to make extra of those items the first time you see them, and store the rest in the freezer so when the recipe comes around again, you just have to reheat it. Just make sure you store everything in good containers and label it so nothing gets lost or ruined.

Prep Strategies: I've shown both prep strategy options from the prep section {page 19}. It can all be completely customized to fit your schedule; this is just to show you what I would do in both cases for each week, so you have a starting point when prepping.

Desserts and Snacks: Dessert isn't a nightly thing for most of us—heck, for some it isn't even a monthly thing. But, just in case you have a sweet tooth or want something a little special, I have two dessert recipes at the end! Snacks are optional, but just know you can always add fresh vegetables, fruits, raw nuts, or extra meat to any meal, or as an additional meal if you need to.

Lastly and most importantly, as always, have fun with this. By now you know that this isn't scary, this is making your life easier and should be making you less stressed out. Just do what you can, when you can.

At a Glance Meal Plans

Week 1

Day 1

Meal 1	Fancy Scrambled Eggs
	Favorite breakfast meat
Meal 2	Roasted Garlic Shrimp with Zucchini Noodles
Meal 3	Lemon Lime Chicken
	Roasted Veggies

Day 2

Meal 1	Strawberry Lemon Muffins
	Eggs or favorite breakfast meat {optional}
Meal 2	Chicken Lettuce Wrap
Meal 3	Ground Pork + Sweet Potato

Day 3

Meal 1	Sweet Potato Broccoli Mix
Meal 2	Leftover Ground Pork + Sweet Potato
	Fresh vegetables {optional}
Meal 3	Tacos + Lettuce Wraps {lettuce wraps optional}
	Serve with your favorite taco toppings
	Side of roasted sweet potatoes, Roasted Veggies, or Broccoli Salad {optional}

Day 4

Meal 1	Strawberry Lemon Muffins
	Eggs or Favorite breakfast meat {optional}
Meal 2	Burrito Bowl
Meal 3	Rosemary Lime Pork Chops
	Serve with side salad and cauliflower rice or white rice {optional}

Day 5

Meal 1	Eggs
	Favorite breakfast meat
	Fresh vegetables
Meal 2	Leftover Rosemary Lime Pork Chops
Meal 3	Spaghetti Squash + Sauce

Day 6

Meal 1	Frittata
Meal 2	Lunchtime Spaghetti Squash
Meal 3	Stir-Fry

Day 7

Meal 1	Banana Pancakes
Meal 2	Leftover Frittata + side salad
Meal 3	Eggplant Stackers
	Side of Roasted Veggies or salad

Week 2

Day 1

Meal 1	Fancy Scrambled Eggs
	Favorite breakfast meat
Meal 2	Tuna + Roasted Sweet Potato
Meal 3	Vegetable Chicken Soup

Day 2

Meal 1	Leftover Vegetable Chicken Soup
Meal 2	Faux Deviled Eggs
	Chicken
	Fresh vegetables
Meal 3	Steak + Eggplant

Day 3

Meal 1	Steak + Eggplant
Meal 2	Chicken Lettuce Wraps
Meal 3	Stir-Fry

Day 4

Meal 1	Eggs
	Favorite breakfast meat
Meal 2	Leftover Stir-Fry
Meal 3	Blueberry Chicken Salad
	Favorite side dish

Day 5

Meal 1	Side salad + Veggies w/ Favorite breakfast Meat
Meal 2	Leftover Blueberry Chicken Salad
Meal 3	Inside-Out Burgers
	Zucchini Sticks or roasted sweet potatoes

Day 6

Meal 1	Frittata
Meal 2	Burrito Bowl
Meal 3	Liz Special

Day 7

Meal 1	Sweet Potato Broccoli Mix
Meal 2	Leftover Liz Special
Meal 3	Fish Cakes
	Side salad or Zucchini Sticks

Week 3

Day 1

Meal 1	Banana Muffins
Meal 2	Leftover Frittata + side salad, or Leftover Fish Cakes
Meal 3	Butternut Squash Soup

Day 2

Meal 1	Fancy Scrambled Eggs
	Favorite breakfast meat
Meal 2	Leftover Soup
Meal 3	Vegetable Chili

Day 3

Meal 1	Banana Muffins
	Faux Deviled Eggs
Meal 2	Leftover Chili
Meal 3	Chicken, Lemon + Broccoli
	Side salad {optional}

Day 4

Meal 1	Sweet Potato Broccoli Mix
Meal 2	Leftover Chicken, Lemon + Broccoli
Meal 3	Tacos with Lettuce Wraps and/or Favorite Toppings
	Roasted Veggies or Zucchini Sticks {optional}

Day 5

Meal 1	Eggs
	Favorite breakfast meat
Meal 2	Tomato Soup + side salad
Meal 3	Liz Special

Day 6

Meal 1	Leftover Liz Special
Meal 2	Leftover Tacos
Meal 3	Breakfast for Dinner!
	You can make: Banana Pancakes, scrambled eggs, breakfast meat, and so on

Day 7

Meal 1	Faux Deviled Eggs
	Fresh Vegetables
Meal 2	Roasted Garlic Shrimp
Meal 3	Rosemary Lime Pork Chops

Week 4

Day 1

Meal 1	Leftover Pancakes
Meal 2	Leftover Rosemary Lime Pork Chops
Meal 3	Chicken, Sausage + Cauliflower

Day 2

Meal 1	Strawberry Lemon Muffins
	Eggs or favorite breakfast meat {optional}
Meal 2	Chicken Lettuce Wraps
Meal 3	Spaghetti Squash + Sauce

Day 3

Meal 1	Faux Deviled Eggs
	Favorite breakfast meat
Meal 2	Leftover Cauliflower Chicken
Meal 3	Sweet Potato + Ground Pork

Day 4

Meal 1	Strawberry Lemon Muffins
	Favorite breakfast meat {optional}
Meal 2	Lunchtime Spaghetti Squash
Meal 3	Blueberry Chicken Salad
	Zucchini Sticks or roasted sweet potatoes {optional}

Day 5

Meal 1	Leftover Blueberry Chicken Salad
Meal 2	Sweet Potato Broccoli Mix
Meal 3	Inside-Out Burgers
	Broccoli Salad

Day 6

Meal 1	Eggs
	Favorite breakfast meat
Meal 2	Burrito Bowl
Meal 3	Eggplant Stackers
	Side salad or favorite side dish {optional}

Day 7

Meal 1	Frittata
Meal 2	Sausage Lettuce Wraps
Meal 3	Lemon Lime Chicken
	Roasted Veggies

Week 1

Meal Plan

Here's the Week 1 Meal Plan! I hope you have fun with this one—you're getting lots of really yummy recipes and a great starting point to help you prep into the next few weeks! And don't forget to check out my Housekeeping Tips for Meal Plans on page 22!

DAY 1

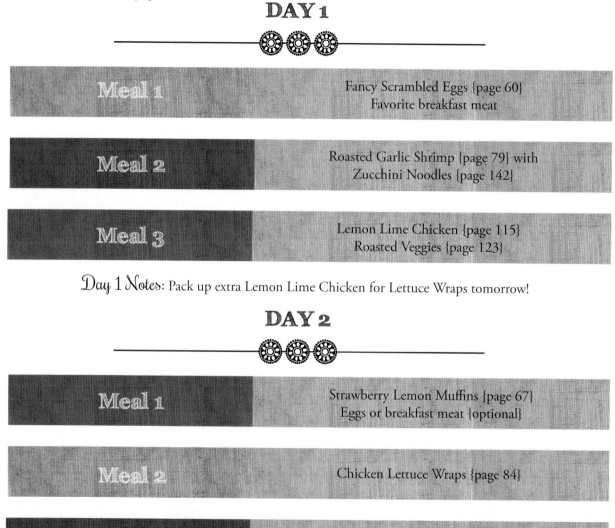

Meal 1	Fancy Scrambled Eggs {page 60} Favorite breakfast meat
Meal 2	Roasted Garlic Shrimp {page 79} with Zucchini Noodles {page 142}
Meal 3	Lemon Lime Chicken {page 115} Roasted Veggies {page 123}

Day 1 Notes: Pack up extra Lemon Lime Chicken for Lettuce Wraps tomorrow!

DAY 2

Meal 1	Strawberry Lemon Muffins {page 67} Eggs or breakfast meat {optional}
Meal 2	Chicken Lettuce Wraps {page 84}
Meal 3	Ground Pork + Sweet Potato {page 106}

Day 2 Notes: Make extra sweet potatoes for Meal 1 tomorrow. And if you're planning to roast fresh broccoli and you haven't yet, you can do it now while you cook your sweet potato!

DAY 3

Meal 1 — Sweet Potato Broccoli Mix {page 70}

Meal 2 — Leftover Ground Pork + Sweet Potato
Fresh vegetables {optional}

Meal 3 — Tacos + Lettuce Wraps {page 121} {lettuce wraps optional},
Served with your favorite taco toppings
Side of roasted sweet potatoes, Roasted Veggies {page 123},
or Broccoli Salad {page 103} {optional}

Day 3 Notes: Set aside extra taco meat for tomorrow's Burrito Bowl.

DAY 4

Meal 1 — Strawberry Lemon Muffins {page 67}
Eggs or breakfast meat {optional}

Meal 2 — Burrito Bowl {page 89}

Meal 3 — Rosemary Lime Pork Chops {page 117}
Serve with side salad and cauliflower rice or white rice {optional}

DAY 5

Meal 1	Eggs, breakfast meat, fresh vegetables
Meal 2	Leftover Rosemary Lime Pork Chops
Meal 3	Spaghetti Squash + Sauce {page 93}

Day 5 Notes: Extra Spaghetti Squash will be used for lunch tomorrow!

DAY 6

Meal 1	Frittata {page 74}
Meal 2	Lunchtime Spaghetti Squash {page 81}
Meal 3	Stir-Fry {page 142}

DAY 7

Meal 1	Banana Pancakes {page 64}
Meal 2	Leftover Frittata + side salad
Meal 3	Eggplant Stackers {page 129} Side of Roasted Veggies {page 123} or salad

Day 7 Notes: Don't forget to prep for tomorrow! See the opposite page for prep strategies.

Prep Strategies
Big Prep Day Method
Big Prep Day

▶ Slice your limes and lemons for the Lemon Lime Chicken and store them in the fridge. Premeasure and store your herb mixture for the Lemon Lime Chicken.

▶ Pre-chop your carrots and zucchini for tomorrow's Roasted Veggies.

▶ Make your Strawberry Lemon Muffins.

▶ Make your Fancy Scrambled Eggs, and store them in the fridge. You can make extra if you'd like to have them for a few days this week.

▶ Make your Roasted Garlic Shrimp for lunch on Day 1. Cut your zucchini into noodles, if using.

▶ Cook your sausage for the Sweet Potato Broccoli Mix {if you're not using a microwaveable sausage like Applegate Farm Pork or Chicken Apple Sausage}. You can also cook up any extra sausage that you'd like to eat for breakfast, lunch, or snacks this week!

▶ Bake your sweet potatoes for Day 2, Meal 3 and Day 3, Meal 1 {see each recipe for more details}.

▶ Hard-boil the eggs you're using this week, and chop any fresh vegetables you'd like to have for easy snacking!

▶ If you have time today, you can make your taco meat for Day 3, Meal 3 and store it in the fridge.

Day One:

▶ Meal 1 and Meal 2 are almost completely done and are really easy!

▶ When you get home and are ready for dinner, juice your lemons. Then assemble the Lemon Lime Chicken and bake.

▶ Chop up your mushrooms and make your Roasted Veggies.

▶ If you haven't and you're making scrambled eggs for breakfast tomorrow morning, you can make those now and store them in the fridge.

▶ Wash and store your lettuce leaves and prep for your Chicken Lettuce Wraps for lunch tomorrow!

Day Two:

▶ Meal 1 and 2 are wicked easy!

▶ When you get home, assemble and cook your Ground Pork + Sweet Potato.

▶ While it's cooking, you can precook your broccoli for tomorrow {if not using a steamfresh bag}.

▶ If you're really in the mood to cook, you can combine your extra sweet potato and broccoli for Day 3 and finely chop up the onion, storing them separately.

Day Three:

▶ Make your Sweet Potato Broccoli Mix.

▶ Meal 2 is a breeze!

▶ If you didn't make your taco meat on your prep day, do it when you get home and store the extra meat.

▶ While you're getting your lettuce leaves together for dinner, pre-chop anything you might need for Day 4 and assemble what you can.

▶ Assemble your Tacos!

Day Four:

▶ Make eggs for breakfast.

▶ If you need to, finish up your Burrito Bowl.

▶ Make your Rosemary Lime Pork Chops.

▶ If you have time while dinner is cooking, you can pre-make Day 5's sauce.

Day Five:

▶ Make Meal 1.

▶ Meal 2 is easy peasy!

▶ When you get home, make your sauce for dinner if you haven't yet. If you have the time and ingredients on hand, make extra sauce and freeze it to make life super easy for you in Week 4 {page 50}!

▶ If you have time, you can also pre-chop your chicken and tomatoes for tomorrow's lunch and make your mayo! You can also make your Frittata if you'd like!

▶ Save the extra spaghetti squash for lunch tomorrow.

▶ Save the leftover sauce for Day 7, Meal 3!

▶ If you're going to veer off course from the meal plan next week, start to plan your meals now!

Day Six:

▶ Make your Frittata if you didn't yesterday.

▶ Make and take your Lunchtime Spaghetti Squash for lunch.

▶ Make your Stir-Fry.

▶ Pre-chop your zucchini and carrots if you're having Roasted Veggies on Day 7.

Day Seven:

▶ Make Banana Pancakes.

▶ Easy lunch today! Just reheat leftovers and make a small salad.

▶ Prep for next week! While you're prepping, you can pre-caramelize your onions and cook your sausage for tonight.

▶ Roast your eggplant for dinner, and while that's going, reheat your leftover sauce and your onions and sausages {or cook them if you need to}.

▶ While your eggplant is roasting, you can roast your vegetables as well!

As-You-Go Prep Method

If you can the day before:

▶ Make hard-boiled eggs for snacking and chop up any veggies you'd like to snack on.

▶ Roast garlic for Day 1, Meal 2.

▶ Slice your lemons and limes for Day 1, Meal 3.

Day One:

▶ Make eggs and breakfast meat.

▶ Quickly cook up your shrimp before you leave the house. If you're in a super big rush and didn't pre-make your roasted garlic, you can skip it and use chopped fresh garlic instead.

▶ When you get home, assemble Lemon Lime Chicken and Roasted Veggies.

▶ If you have time, you can make your Strawberry Lemon Muffins while the chicken cooks and bake them while you eat dinner!

Day Two:

▶ Make breakfast.

▶ Take leftovers and other veggies and lettuce leaves for Chicken Lettuce Wraps for lunch.

▶ When you get home, make your sweet potato and meat. Make extra sweet potatoes for breakfast tomorrow.

▶ While that's cooking, precook your broccoli for Day 3 {if you're not using a steamfresh bag} and pre-chop your onions. Store the sweet potatoes and broccoli together and the onions separately.

Day Three:

▶ Finish making and assembling your Sweet Potato Broccoli Mix.

▶ Take your leftovers with you for lunch.

▶ When you get home, make your Tacos and save the extra taco meat.

▶ Chop up your lettuce and veggies for Day 4's salad, and precook whatever meat you'd like to have with it.

Day Four:

▶ Make your eggs and serve them with muffins.

▶ Assemble your Burrito Bowl using leftover taco meat.

▶ Make Rosemary Lime Pork Chops for dinner.

Day Five:

▶ Make your eggs and breakfast meat, and chop any veggies you'd like with it.

▶ Take leftovers with you for lunch.

▶ When you get home, make your Spaghetti Squash + Sauce, and reserve some extra sauce for Day 7, Meal 3. If you have the time and ingredients, plan to make extra for Week 4's dinner and for Day 7 Meal 3 and freeze.

▶ Save extra spaghetti squash for Meal 2 tomorrow.

▶ If you have time while everything is cooking, chop up your lettuce for Day 6.

▶ If you're going to veer off course from the meal plan next week, plan your meals now!

Day Six:

▶ Make your Frittata.

▶ Assemble Lunchtime Spaghetti Squash.

▶ Make your Stir-Fry.

Day Seven:

▶ Make your Banana Pancakes!

▶ Have leftovers for lunch.

▶ Make Eggplant Stackers for dinner.

▶ If you have time to prep for next week, do it today!

Shopping List

Meat, Poultry, Fish, or Chicken:

- ▶ Favorite breakfast meat {sausage, bacon, and so on}
- ▶ Sausages
- ▶ Shrimp
- ▶ Boneless, skinless chicken breast
- ▶ Ground pork
- ▶ Ground beef
- ▶ Boneless, skinless pork chops

Fresh Ingredients:

- ▶ Bananas
- ▶ Large eggplant
- ▶ Zucchini
- ▶ Carrots
- ▶ Onions
- ▶ Mushrooms {I normally get 12-ounce packs, but get whatever is the most economical.}
- ▶ Spaghetti squash
- ▶ Cauliflower {optional}
- ▶ Tomatoes
- ▶ Sweet potatoes
- ▶ Lettuce {I like romaine lettuce}
- ▶ Eggs
- ▶ Lemons
- ▶ Limes
- ▶ Garlic
- ▶ Veggies to snack on this week

Frozen:

- ▶ 1 {8-oz.} bag pepper strips
- ▶ Assorted mixed vegetables
- ▶ Diced strawberries {or whatever is cheapest}
- ▶ Spinach or kale
- ▶ Green beans
- ▶ Broccoli

Other:

- ▶ Canned diced tomatoes
- ▶ Canned crushed tomatoes
- ▶ Favorite fat
- ▶ Any dried herbs you might be out of
- ▶ Almond flour
- ▶ Coconut flour
- ▶ Olive oil

Week 2

Meal Plan

Week 2 Meal Plan! Look at you, you're all fancy over there with your meal planning and prepping. It's official: you're one of the cool kids now. So go get to eating these ridiculously yummy meals this week! And don't forget to check out my Housekeeping Tips for Meal Plans on page 22!

DAY 1

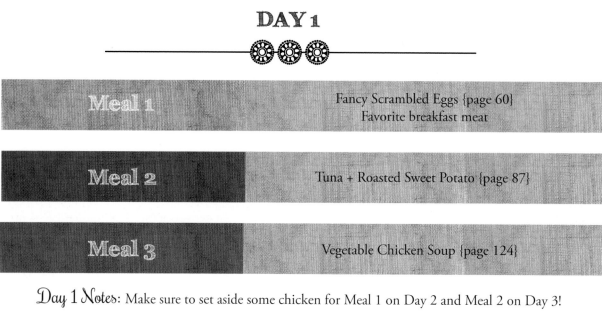

Meal 1 — Fancy Scrambled Eggs {page 60}
Favorite breakfast meat

Meal 2 — Tuna + Roasted Sweet Potato {page 87}

Meal 3 — Vegetable Chicken Soup {page 124}

Day 1 Notes: Make sure to set aside some chicken for Meal 1 on Day 2 and Meal 2 on Day 3!

DAY 2

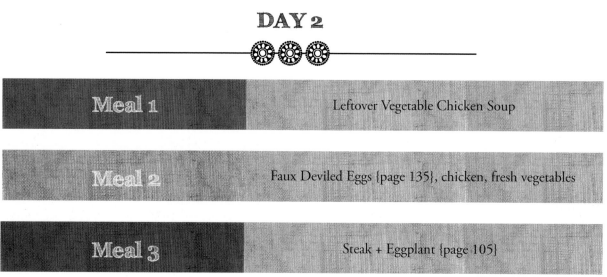

Meal 1 — Leftover Vegetable Chicken Soup

Meal 2 — Faux Deviled Eggs {page 135}, chicken, fresh vegetables

Meal 3 — Steak + Eggplant {page 105}

Day 2 Notes: When cutting up vegetables for Meal 3, you can cut up a few extra for your Lettuce Wraps on Day 3!

DAY 3

Meal 1	Leftover Steak + Eggplant
Meal 2	Chicken Lettuce Wraps {page 84}
Meal 3	Stir-Fry {page 142}

DAY 4

Meal 1	Eggs Favorite breakfast meat
Meal 2	Leftover Stir-Fry
Meal 3	Blueberry Chicken Salad {page 118} Favorite side dish

DAY 5

Meal 1	Veggies w/ favorite breakfast meat
Meal 2	Leftover Blueberry Chicken Salad
Meal 3	Inside-Out Burgers {page 96} Zucchini Sticks {page 100} or roasted sweet potatoes

Day 5 Notes: Make extra burgers to use for Burrito Bowl tomorrow. You can also cook up extra Zucchini Sticks or a roasted sweet potato to add on top to make things interesting! If you are making roasted sweet potatoes, cook extra up to use for Day 7, Meal 1!

DAY 6

Meal 1	Frittata {page 74}
Meal 2	Burrito Bowl {page 89}
Meal 3	Liz Special {page 99}

Day 6 Notes: Make sure you take time to relax today!

DAY 7

Meal 1	Sweet Potato Broccoli Mix {page 70}
Meal 2	Leftover Liz Special
Meal 3	Fish Cakes {page 126} Side salad or Zucchini Sticks {page 100}

Day 7 Notes: Don't forget to prep for tomorrow! See the opposite page for prep strategies.

Prep Strategies
Big Prep Day Method
Prep Day

▶ Make your Fancy Scrambled Eggs for tomorrow's breakfast, and make extra if you'd like to do eggs another morning early this week instead of leftovers.

▶ Make your chicken stock and make sure to cut up or shred your chicken.

▶ Heat up your Vegetable Chicken Soup for dinner, or if you need to, make it now!

▶ Roast your sweet potatoes and feel free to roast up extra to add to your Chicken Lettuce Wraps.

▶ Pre-chop your steak for Day 2, Meal 3.

▶ Hard-boil as many eggs as you'd like for the week. Chop up any veggies you'd like for snacking this week!

▶ Make a few batches of mayo and store in the fridge.

▶ If you're making Zucchini Sticks this week, you can premix your dry ingredients and store until ready to use.

Day One:

▶ Reheat your eggs and make your favorite breakfast meat.

▶ Assemble your Tuna + Roasted Sweet Potato.

▶ Heat up your Vegetable Chicken Soup for dinner or make it now.

Day Two:

▶ Breakfast is easy!

▶ While your soup is heating, make sure to gather toppings for the Faux Deviled Eggs. Pack up your lunch.

▶ Make your Steak + Eggplant.

▶ While your vegetables are roasting, prep your Chicken Lettuce Wraps for Day 3!

Day Three:

▶ Easy breakfast!

▶ Pack up the items for your Chicken Lettuce Wraps.

▶ Stir-Fry for dinner! Super easy. :}

▶ If you're having scrambled eggs for Meal 1 tomorrow, you can make those tonight!

Day Four:

▶ Make breakfast.

▶ Pack up leftovers for lunch.

▶ Make Blueberry Chicken Salad using the mayo you made on prep day.

▶ Make your favorite side dish.

▶ Chop up your lettuce for salad on Day 5. Precook your breakfast meat if you'd like!

▶ If you have time, you can either pre-make your mashed carrots, or you can make your entire filling for the Inside-Out Burgers.

Day Five:

▶ Make breakfast.

▶ Pack up leftovers for lunch!

▶ Make your Inside-Out Burgers and a side dish of choice.

▶ If you'd like, you can also make your Frittata tonight.

▶ If you're going to veer off course from the meal plan next week, start to plan your meals now!

Day Six:

▶ Reheat or make your Frittata.

▶ Make your Burrito Bowl for lunch, using the extra burgers for the meat.

▶ Make the Liz Special for dinner, saving the leftovers for Meal 2 tomorrow.

Day 7:

▶ Make your Sweet Potato Broccoli Mix for breakfast.

▶ Make your Fish Cakes for dinner with your side dish of choice!.

▶ Prep for next week's meals!

As-You-Go Prep method

If you can the day before:

▶ Make some hard-boiled eggs for the week.

▶ Pre-make your scrambled eggs for tomorrow.

▶ Roast up some sweet potatoes.

▶ Make your chicken stock. {That's probably the most important step.}

Day 1:

▶ Reheat or make your eggs and breakfast meat.

▶ Make your Tuna + Roasted Sweet Potato.

▶ Make your Vegetable Chicken Soup when you get home. Make sure to save leftovers for breakfast tomorrow!

Day 2:

▶ Breakfast is easy!

▶ Pack up lunch.

▶ Make your Steak + Eggplant, saving the leftovers for breakfast tomorrow.

▶ Prep for Meal 2 tomorrow by getting your lettuce leaves ready and packed up.

Day 3:

▶ Breakfast is easy!

▶ Take your lettuce wraps with you.

▶ Dinner is wicked easy!

▶ If you have time, precook your breakfast meat for tomorrow.

Day 4:

▶ Make breakfast.

▶ Lunch is extremely easy today!

▶ Make the Blueberry Chicken Salad and your favorite side dish.

▶ If you have time, you can pre-chop your lettuce for breakfast tomorrow.

Day 5:

▶ Make breakfast.

▶ Lunch is super easy!

▶ Make your Inside-Out Burgers. {If you don't have time to make stuffed burgers, just make regular burgers.}

▶ If you're going to veer off course from the meal plan next week, plan your meals now!

Day 6:

▶ Make your Frittata.

▶ Use leftover burgers to make your Burrito Bowl.

▶ Make the Liz Special for dinner and save the leftovers for tomorrow!

Day 7:

▶ Make your Sweet Potato Broccoli Mix.

▶ Lunch is easy!

▶ Make your Fish Cakes and your side dish of choice.

▶ Do any prep work you can for tomorrow.

Shopping List

Meat, Poultry, Fish, or Chicken*:

▶ Favorite breakfast meat {sausage, bacon, and so on}

▶ Sausages

▶ Bacon

▶ Ground pork

▶ Ground beef

▶ Steak {your favorite cut}

▶ Whole chicken {if making your own stock; if not, just buy chicken breast}

▶ Canned tuna {if using}

Fresh Ingredients:

▶ Eggplant

▶ Zucchini

▶ Carrots

▶ Onions

▶ Mushrooms {I normally get 12-ounce packs, but get whatever is the most economical.}

▶ Celery

▶ Cucumbers

▶ Tomatoes

▶ Sweet potatoes

▶ Lettuce {I like romaine lettuce}

▶ Bell pepper

▶ Eggs

▶ Lemons

▶ Veggies to snack on this week

Frozen:

▶ Assorted mixed vegetables

▶ Spinach or kale

▶ Broccoli

▶ Blueberries

Other:

▶ Favorite fat

▶ Any dried herbs you might be out of

▶ Almond flour

▶ Coconut flour

▶ Olive oil

▶ Chicken stock

*Because the Fish Cakes are for Day 7, Meal 3, you'll want to purchase the fish when you shop for Week 3 so your fish is super fresh!

Week 3

Meal Plan

Meal Plan for Week 3! Can you believe you're now considered a pro at this? I know, I know, this is amazing. This week is going to have a few repeats for you meal-wise, which actually makes your life a little easier because you already know your way around them! So go cook like a champ and have a great week! P.S. don't forget to check out my Housekeeping Tips for Meal Plans on page 22!

DAY 1

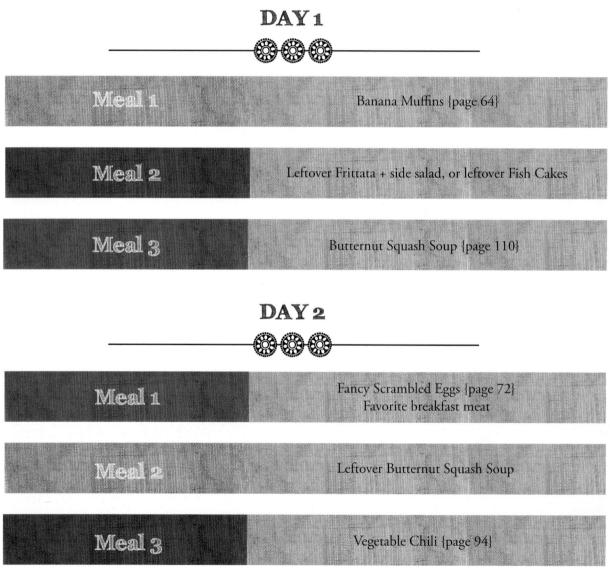

Meal 1	Banana Muffins {page 64}
Meal 2	Leftover Frittata + side salad, or leftover Fish Cakes
Meal 3	Butternut Squash Soup {page 110}

DAY 2

Meal 1	Fancy Scrambled Eggs {page 72} Favorite breakfast meat
Meal 2	Leftover Butternut Squash Soup
Meal 3	Vegetable Chili {page 94}

Day 2 Notes: Save extra Chili to use as optional topping for Taco Night on Day 4.

DAY 3

Meal 1	Banana Muffins {page 69} Faux Deviled Eggs {page 135}

Meal 2	Leftover Chili

Meal 3	Chicken, Lemon + Broccoli {page 112} Side salad {optional}

Day 3 Notes: You can make extra broccoli now and use it for Day 4, Meal 1. If you're going to roast fresh broccoli, you can also roast your sweet potatoes for Day 4, Meal 1!

DAY 4

Meal 1	Sweet Potato Broccoli Mix {page 70}

Meal 2	Leftover Chicken, Lemon + Broccoli

Meal 3	Tacos {page 121} + Lettuce Wraps and/or favorite toppings Roasted Veggies {page 123} or Zucchini Sticks {page 100} {optional}

DAY 5

Meal 1	Eggs Favorite breakfast meat

Meal 2	Tomato Soup {page 82} + side salad

Meal 3	Liz Special {page 99}

Day 5 Notes: For something special, make some extra breakfast meat and add it to the top of your salad today!

DAY 6

Meal 1	Leftover Liz Special
Meal 2	Leftover Tacos
Meal 3	Breakfast for Dinner! Your choice: Banana Pancakes {page 64}, Fancy Scrambled Eggs {page 72}, breakfast meat, and so on

Day 6 Notes: Just a friendly reminder to relax and unwind a little!

DAY 7

Meal 1	Faux Deviled Eggs {page 135} Fresh vegetables
Meal 2	Roasted Garlic Shrimp {page 79} + Zucchini Noodles {page 142} {optional}
Meal 3	Rosemary Lime Pork Chops {page 117}

Day 7 Notes: Don't forget to prep for tomorrow! See the opposite page for prep strategies.

Prep Strategies
Big Prep Day Method

Prep Day

▶ Make your Banana Muffins.

▶ Make your Fancy Scrambled Eggs.

▶ Make your Vegetable Chili. {If you have time and space, make a double batch and freeze it for another day!}

▶ Make hard-boiled eggs for Faux Deviled Eggs, and any extra you might want for the rest of the week.

▶ Chop up any vegetables you'd like to have throughout the week.

▶ Caramelize your onions for Day 1, Meal 3.

▶ Chop up your lettuce for Day 3.

▶ If you want, you can make Day 1, Meal 3's soup today.

Day One:

▶ Breakfast and lunch are easy today!

▶ If you need to, make the soup for Meal 3 or reheat it.

▶ Remember to pack up extras for Meal 2 tomorrow!

Day Two:

▶ Reheat your eggs and make your favorite breakfast meat.

▶ Lunch is easy!

▶ Reheat your Vegetable Chili and chop up any toppings you'd like {avocado, onions, mayo, raw cheese, and so on}.

▶ If you have time while your Vegetable Chili is reheating, you can cut up your chicken and cook your broccoli for tomorrow. If you make your broccoli tonight, make some extra for Day 4, Meal 1!

Day Three:

▶ Breakfast and lunch are super easy!

▶ Make your Chicken, Lemon, + Broccoli and a side salad or favorite side dish.

▶ If you have time and want to, you can pre-make Day 4, Meal 1 tonight. And if you don't want to roast your sweet potato or don't have the time, you can bake it instead in the microwave, chop it up when cooled, and add into the Sweet Potato Broccoli Mix as normal.

Day Four:

▶ Make your Sweet Potato Broccoli Mix. {See note on sweet potato on previous page.}

▶ Meal 2 is easy!

▶ Make Tacos, your favorite side dish, and any toppings!

▶ While the Tacos are simmering, you can quickly put together your Tomato Soup for lunch tomorrow and prep your salad.

▶ Save the leftover Tacos for Meal 2 on Day 6.

Day Five:

▶ Make your eggs and breakfast meat.

▶ If you haven't yet, quickly put together your soup and salad.

▶ Make your Liz Special for Meal 3.

▶ If you're going to veer off course from the meal plan next week, start to plan your meals now!

Day Six:

▶ Meal 1 and Meal 2 are super easy!

▶ Make your favorite breakfast items tonight for Meal 3. {Just make sure to make extra pancakes to have next week, Meal 1 Day 1.}

Day Seven:

▶ Meal 1 is easy!

▶ Prep for tomorrow.

▶ Make your Roasted Garlic Shrimp for lunch with Zucchini Noodles.

▶ Make your Rosemary Lime Pork Chops for dinner! You can serve it with cauliflower rice, white rice, or eat it as is!

As-You-Go Prep Strategy

If you can the day before:

▶ Make your hard-boiled eggs.

▶ Make Banana Muffins.

Day One:

▶ Make your muffins if you need to.

▶ Meal 2 is easy!

▶ Make your Butternut Squash Soup and save the leftovers for Meal 2 tomorrow.

Day Two:

▶ Make your eggs and meat. {If you don't want to spend the extra time making Fancy Scrambled Eggs, make them whatever way is quickest for you!}

▶ Meal 2 is easy!

▶ Make your Vegetable Chili. {If you have time and the ingredients, you could plan to make a double batch and freeze the extra for a dinner in the near future!}

Day Three:

▶ Meal 1 and Meal 2 are easy!

▶ Make your Chicken, Lemon, + Broccoli. {If you can, cook extra broccoli for Meal 1 tomorrow.}

▶ If you know you won't have time to roast a sweet potato either tonight or tomorrow night, you can quickly cook it in the microwave while Meal 3 is cooking, to make tomorrow even easier.

Day Four:

▶ Make Sweet Potato Broccoli Mix.

▶ Meal 2 is easy!

▶ Make your Tacos and Favorite side dish with your favorite toppings {toppings and side dish are optional}.

▶ If you have time while your Tacos are simmering away, you can quickly make the Tomato Soup tonight for Meal 2 tomorrow!

Day Five:

▶ Make Meal 1.

▶ Make Meal 2 if you need to.

▶ Make the Liz Special for Meal 3.

▶ If you're going to veer off course from the meal plan next week, plan your meals now!

Day Six:

▶ Meals 1 and 2 are easy!

▶ Have your favorite breakfast items for Meal 3! Just remember to make extra pancakes and store them in the fridge for Meal 1, Day 1 of next week!

Day Seven:

▶ Make your Faux Deviled Eggs.

▶ Make your Roasted Garlic Shrimp with optional Zucchini Noodles. If you don't have time or want to roast garlic, you can swap it out for fresh garlic instead.

▶ Do any prep work you'd like to for next week.

▶ Make your Rosemary Lime Pork Chops for dinner. You can serve it with cauliflower rice, white rice, or eat it as is!

Shopping List

Meat, Poultry, Fish, or Chicken*:

▶ Favorite breakfast meat {sausage, bacon, and so on}

▶ Sausages

▶ White fish for Week 2, Day 7, Meal 3

▶ Boneless, skinless, chicken breast

▶ Ground pork

▶ Ground beef

▶ Boneless, skinless pork chops

Fresh Ingredients:

▶ Bananas

▶ Large eggplant

▶ Zucchini

▶ Butternut squash

▶ Carrots

▶ Onions

▶ Mushrooms {I normally get 12-ounce packs, but get whatever is the most economical.}

▶ Spaghetti squash

▶ Cauliflower {optional}

▶ Tomatoes

▶ Sweet potatoes

▶ Lettuce {I like romaine lettuce}

▶ Eggs

▶ Lemons

▶ Garlic

▶ Veggies to snack on this week

Frozen:

▶ 1 {8-oz.} bag pepper strips

▶ Assorted mixed vegetables

▶ Spinach or kale

▶ Broccoli

Other:

▶ Canned diced tomatoes

▶ Canned crushed tomatoes

▶ Favorite fat

▶ Any dried herbs you might be out of

▶ Almond flour

▶ Coconut flour

▶ Olive oil

*Because the shrimp is for Day 7 Meal 2, you'll want to purchase the shrimp when you shop for Week 4 so your shrimp is super fresh!

Week 4

Meal Plan

Week 4's Meal Plan! I think it's time—you're totally ready to plan out your own meal plan for next week. I think this is what we could call super exciting or epic. I personally think you could even get away with wicked epic! Remember around Day 5 to start planning your meals and checking out your store circulars! And don't forget to check out my Housekeeping Tips for Meal Plans on page 22!

DAY 1

Meal 1	Leftover Pancakes
Meal 2	Leftover Rosemary Lime Pork Chops
Meal 3	Cauliflower Chicken {page 109}

Day 1 Notes:

- When making meal 3, you can skip the roasting of the vegetable part because it's already done! Just add the vegetables in toward the end to let them reheat a little bit!
- Cook extra chicken with the Cauliflower Chicken and set aside to use for Day 2, Meal 2

DAY 2

Meal 1	Strawberry Lemon Muffins {page 67} Eggs or favorite breakfast meat {optional}
Meal 2	Chicken Lettuce Wraps {page 84}
Meal 3	Spaghetti Squash + Sauce {page 93}

Day 2 Notes: Save extra spaghetti squash to use on Day 4, Meal 2!

DAY 3

Meal 1
Breakfast meat
Faux Deviled Eggs {page 135}

Meal 2
Leftover Cauliflower Chicken

Meal 3
Ground Pork + Sweet Potato {page 106}

DAY 4

Meal 1
Strawberry Lemon Muffins {page 67}
Breakfast meat {optional}

Meal 2
Lunchtime Spaghetti Squash {page 81}

Meal 3
Blueberry Chicken Salad {page 118}
Zucchini Sticks or roasted sweet potatoes {optional}

DAY 5

Meal 1
Leftover Blueberry Chicken Salad

Meal 2
Sweet Potato Broccoli Mix {page 70}

Meal 3
Inside-Out Burgers {page 96}
Broccoli Salad {page 103}

DAY 6

Meal 1	Eggs Favorite breakfast meat
Meal 2	Burrito Bowl {page 89}
Meal 3	Eggplant Stackers {page 129} Side salad or favorite side dish {optional}

Day 6 Notes: Make extra sausage tonight to use for Meal 2 tomorrow!

DAY 7

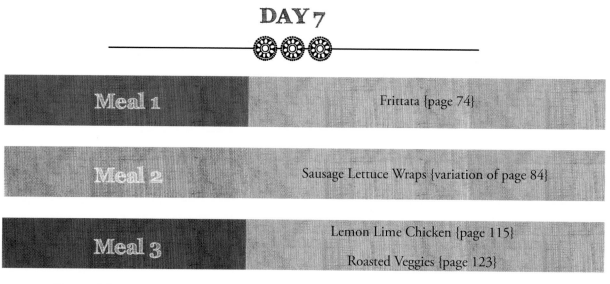

Meal 1	Frittata {page 74}
Meal 2	Sausage Lettuce Wraps {variation of page 84}
Meal 3	Lemon Lime Chicken {page 115} Roasted Veggies {page 123}

Day 7 Notes: Don't forget to prep for tomorrow! See the opposite page for prep strategies.

Prep Strategies
Big Prep Day Method

Prep Day

▶ Make Strawberry Lemon Muffins.

▶ Make your sauce for the Spaghetti Squash, if you don't have any stored in the freezer.

▶ Roast up your cauliflower and carrots for Meal 3 tomorrow. You can roast up extra vegetables here to have as a side dish one day this week, or to just snack on!

▶ If you'd like to and you have time, you can pre-bake your sweet potato for Day 3, Meal 3 while your cauliflower and carrots are roasting! While you're at it, you can cook up a few extra to have for snacking and a side dish this week!

▶ Hard-boil as many eggs as you'd like for the week, and chop up any fresh vegetables for snacking throughout the week.

▶ If you're making Zucchini Sticks on Day 4, Meal 3, you can pre-make the coating now, and then store it until you're ready to use it.

Day One:

▶ Meal 1 and 2 are easy!

▶ Assemble Meal 3, making sure to cook extra chicken for Meal 2 tomorrow!

▶ Prep your lettuce leaves for your Chicken Lettuce Wraps tomorrow. Cut up and pack up whatever veggies you'd like with it, along with your chicken!

Day Two:

▶ Meal 1 and 2 are a breeze!

▶ Finish making Meal 3, or just reheat everything.

▶ Set aside extra sauce for Day 6.

▶ Save extra spaghetti squash for Meal 2 on Day 4.

Day Three:

▶ Meal 1 and 2 are wicked easy!

▶ Make your sweet potato and ground pork.

▶ While Meal 3 is cooking, you can make your Lunchtime Spaghetti Squash; just leave out the mayo and store it separately. Then add it in right before eating to ensure nothing gets soggy!

▶ If you have time today, you can pre-mash your carrots and store in fridge for Meal 3 on Day 5!

Day Four:

▶ Once again, Meals 1 and 2 are super easy!

▶ Make your Blueberry Chicken Salad and side dish of choice.

▶ Save extra Blueberry Chicken Salad for Meal 1 tomorrow.

▶ If you have time and don't have one cooked up yet, cook up your sweet potato for Meal 2 tomorrow, as well as your sausage. {Cook extra sausage to have for Meal 3 tomorrow as well, if you're serving the broccoli salad as a side dish.}

Day Five:

▶ Meal 1 is easy!

▶ Finish making Meal 2.

▶ Make Inside-Out Burgers and a side dish of choice.

▶ Save the leftover burgers for Meal 2 tomorrow.

▶ Start to plan your meals now for next week!

Day Six:

▶ Make Meal 1 and assemble Meal 2.

▶ Roast up your eggplant and reheat the sauce for the Eggplant Stackers. Cook the sausage and onions if you need to. When cooking the sausages, cook extra for Meal 2 tomorrow.

▶ Serve with your favorite side dish.

Day Seven:

▶ Make your Frittata.

▶ Meal 2 is easy!

▶ Cook Lemon Lime Chicken and Roasted Veggies.

▶ Prep for next week.

As-You-Go Prep Method

If you can the day before:

▶ Roast up vegetables for Meal 3 tomorrow.

▶ Make Strawberry Lemon Muffins.

▶ Cook up any hard-boiled eggs you'll need and chop up any fresh vegetables you'd like to have to snack on this week.

Day One:

▶ Meal 1 and 2 are easy!

▶ Make Cauliflower Chicken. Cook up extra chicken and store it for Meal 2 tomorrow.

Day Two:

▶ Meal 1 and 2 are easy!

▶ Make Spaghetti Squash + Sauce, saving both the extra sauce and spaghetti squash for other meals this week.

▶ While the spaghetti squash is cooking, bake your sweet potato for tomorrow's Meal 3 and Day 5 Meal 2.

Day Three:

▶ Meal 1 and Meal 2 are a breeze. Enjoy!

▶ Finish the sweet potato and pork.

▶ If you have time, make the spaghetti squash and tomorrow's Meal 2. {Just don't add the mayo in; store it separately and add in before eating to ensure nothing gets soggy! }

Day Four:

▶ Meals 1 and 2 are pretty much ready to go!

▶ Make Blueberry Chicken Salad and side dish of choice. Remember to save the extra salad!

▶ If you have time while your side dish is cooking, you can make the filling for the Inside-Out Burgers {Meal 3 tomorrow}.

▶ If you have time, you can make the Sweet Potato Broccoli Mix tonight!

Day Five:

▶ Meal 1 is ready to go!

▶ Meal 2 is almost done—just finish making it if you need to.

▶ Make your Inside-Out Burgers and side dish for Meal 3. Remember to save the extra burger for your Burrito Bowl tomorrow!

▶ If you're going to veer off course from the meal plan next week, start to plan your meals now!

Day Six:

▶ Meal 1 is easy to cook!

▶ Assemble your Burrito Bowl for Meal 2.

▶ Roast up your eggplant and make Eggplant Stackers {using the Spaghetti Squash + Sauce leftovers} and your favorite side dish.

▶ Remember to make extra sausage for Day 7, Meal 2.

Day Seven:

▶ Make your Frittata.

▶ Make your sausage lettuce wraps.

▶ Do any prep work you can for next week.

▶ Make your Lemon Lime Chicken and Roasted Veggies!

Shopping List

Meat, Poultry, Fish, or Chicken:

▶ Favorite breakfast meat {sausage, bacon, and so on}

▶ Sausages

▶ Boneless, skinless, chicken breast

▶ Shrimp {For Week 3, Day 7, Meal 2}

▶ Ground pork

▶ Ground beef

Fresh Ingredients:

▶ Large eggplant

▶ Zucchini

▶ Carrots

▶ Onions

▶ Mushrooms {I normally get 12-ounce packs, but get whatever is the most economical.}

▶ Spaghetti squash

▶ Cauliflower

▶ Tomatoes

▶ Sweet potatoes

▶ Lettuce {I like romaine lettuce}

▶ Eggs

▶ Lemons

▶ Limes

▶ Veggies to snack on this week

Frozen:

▶ Assorted mixed vegetables

▶ Diced strawberries {or whatever is cheapest}

▶ Spinach or kale

▶ Broccoli

▶ Green beans

Other:

▶ Canned diced tomatoes

▶ Canned crushed tomatoes

▶ Favorite fat

▶ Any dried herbs you might be out of

▶ Almond flour

▶ Coconut flour

▶ Olive oil

Recipes

The recipes in this book are some of my favorites that I've created so far. I'm not even joking right now—wait until you try the Fish Cakes or the Cauliflower Chicken {or dare I say the Maple Bacon Cookies?}! Remember that these recipes are only guidelines. If you don't have a particular vegetable, leave it out or add what you have on hand. Don't go out and buy just one ingredient for a recipe; use what you have and make it work. And just to make life a little easier for you, I included a few cooking tips.

Helpful Hints

▶ Seasonings: The dried herbs are more like suggestions. If you don't like thyme but prefer basil or oregano, just swap the spice out. And if you've got a green thumb {I'm officially jealous if you do}, then go for the fresh herbs. Just remember that dried herbs are normally double the strength flavor-wise than fresh herbs. So if a recipe calls for 1 tablespoon of dried basil, you're probably going to have to use 2 tablespoons {or a little more} of fresh basil.

If you grow your own herbs, you can also dry them to make your own dried herb blends. You can even store them in the freezer! Just Google "how to freeze your favorite herbs" for specific instructions, since some herbs vary in how they should be frozen or stored.

▶ As far as the "fat of choice" you'll see in most recipes, that's exactly what it sounds like. You can use any fat that makes you happy here {e.g. ghee, grass-fed butter, coconut oil, bacon fat, duck fat, and so on}.

▶ Frozen fruits and vegetables: Often you'll see frozen fruits and vegetables listed in these recipes. The main reason for this is that they're normally less expensive than their fresh counterparts, and they last longer. You can have a bag of frozen blueberries in your freezer for months without worrying about it going bad, whereas you'll have those fresh blueberries for a few weeks at most. The other reason is that it's nice to have your favorite fruits and vegetables on hand for easy, quick cooking. Let's say you have a hankering for a Raspberry Mug Cake or Blueberry Chicken Salad at the most random time possible. By having these small items on hand, you'll be ready for that sudden craving without screwing up your budget for the week! However, if you're an "I only like fresh fruits and vegetables" kinda person, don't fear: you can just swap the frozen ones for fresh ones!

▶ Canned tomatoes: When you're purchasing these, make sure you're getting as close to "tomato-only" as possible. Also, make sure you look for brands that are "no salt added," especially when it comes to diced tomatoes. And don't go for the flavored versions of these tomatoes because they generally have sugar and other additives. Don't like canned products? Just swap out the canned for fresh tomatoes whenever a recipe calls for them.

▶ Maple syrup, raw honey, and vanilla extract: These are lumped together because they follow the same guidelines. You want the best quality you can afford of each. With maple syrup it's kind of backwards, because the Grade B syrups are a higher quality than the Grade A. You want to try and get a Dark Amber Grade A syrup or a Grade B. The closer to local you can get, the better. With honey you just want to make sure it's raw, and you should try to get a local brand. Some people think it can help to build up a small amount of immunity to pollen-based allergies. And last, vanilla extract is the same as the others; the higher the quality, the better! Read the ingredients on them, because some contain an alcohol base and some don't. It just depends on your preference.

Breakfast

Banana Pancakes

Are you ready for a weird fact? I only like banana when it's mixed into foods that are cooked. Super weird, right? I can't eat a banana just to eat a banana, but these Banana Pancakes? I can't stop eating them. They're that good! Now here's the little insider's secret to making a Paleo pancake: smaller is better. I know, I know, it's way more impressive to have a huge pancake, but if you want them to cook evenly, be easy to flip, and stay together while flipping, you need to go smaller. Plus, it's easier to sneak one if they're smaller, because no one will know that it's missing. You're welcome. ;}

Also, I know I have these listed for breakfast in the meal plan, but don't be afraid to use them as a breakfast-for-dinner item, or even as a dessert!

Ingredients

2 very ripe bananas, mashed

3 eggs

¾ cup almond flour

¼ cup coconut flour

½ cup water

1 Tbsp. raw honey, melted

1 Tbsp. vanilla extract

1 tsp. cinnamon

pinch of salt

fat of choice

Serves: 2–4 people

How To

▶ In a large bowl, mash up your bananas with a fork.

▶ Add in the rest of your ingredients, except for fat of choice, remembering to crack your eggs in a separate bowl first before adding them into your mixing bowl.

▶ Mix everything in your bowl well.

▶ Heat a large skillet with your favorite fat over medium to medium-high heat.

▶ Use a tablespoon measuring spoon, pour your pancake batter into the pan. In my large skillet I can fit four pancakes without overcrowding.

▶ Let your pancakes cook on one side for a few minutes, until they start to bubble just a little on top and are cooked and golden on the bottom. Then flip and finish cooking. Boom, you've got a pancake! Or four!

▶ If you're making a huge batch, keep a plate covered with aluminum foil to keep the pancakes warm.

▶ Serve with your favorite fat and a good-quality maple syrup if you'd like, and then enjoy!

Author's Note: If you don't let the pancakes cook enough on the first side and try to flip them too early, they could fall apart a bit. But don't worry, just go with it and re-flip it after the other side has cooked through. It might not look like the prettiest pancake, but it'll still taste amazing!

Strawberry Lemon Muffins

These muffins have been my baby throughout this book. I don't know why, but they've been my favorite thing to develop. Probably because of the mix of lemons, strawberries, and muffins—you know how it goes. Anyway, these are amazing. They're filling, tangy, and sweet, all at the same time. They're fantastic for breakfast, but are also great as a snack. Or heck, if you throw some chocolate chips in these, you'll have a really fun, interesting dessert on your hands! Here's the skinny on the strawberries for these yummy little bad boys: I used pre-diced frozen strawberries. They cost the same for me as either sliced or whole strawberries and they're literally no work as they're ready to go. But you can use any kind of frozen strawberries, or you can even get crazy and use fresh ones! Whatever you have on hand will work.

Note: Because everyone's level of hunger is different, you might need to still have some eggs with these in the morning, or a few slices of bacon! For me personally, around two muffins and my morning cup of bulletproof coffee does me just fine until lunch!

Ingredients

1 cup almond flour
¼ cup coconut flour
4 eggs
¼ cup maple syrup
juice from two lemons {about 6 Tbsp.}
½ cup frozen diced strawberries
1 Tbsp. good-quality vanilla extract
1 tsp. cinnamon
pinch of salt

How To

▶ Preheat your oven to 375°F.

▶ In a large mixing bowl, add in your almond flour, coconut flour, and eggs. Mix.

▶ Add the rest of your ingredients and mix well.

▶ Either line your muffin tin with liners, or grease the tins liberally with your favorite fat.

▶ Scoop an even amount into your muffin tins. {I have a 12-muffin tin that's slightly deep, so I can fill up between 7–8 muffins with this recipe.} These muffins don't really rise, so feel free to fill them all the way to the top.

▶ Bake for 25–30 minutes, or until they are golden brown on top and set in the center.

▶ Let cool and enjoy!

Makes: 6–8 muffins

Banana Muffins

Banana Muffins! Seriously, there should be a happy dance for these things. To be honest, the main reason I think they're perfect for this book is because we've already got Banana Pancakes. So what happens when you have extra bananas? If you thought "make muffins" then you were correct! These will stretch and they're beyond delightful, and it's pretty hard to eat just one! I used a standard-sized muffin tin for these, but you can play around with different sizes and cooking times for something fun!

Ingredients

2 almost over-ripe bananas

1½ cups almond flour

3 large eggs

4 Tbsp. melted butter or coconut oil

2 tsp. vanilla extract

2 tsp. ground cinnamon

pinch of salt

¼ cup almonds, finely chopped

How To

▶ Preheat your oven to 350°F.

▶ With a fork, mash your bananas in a bowl very well.

▶ Add in the rest of your ingredients and mix well. Remember to crack your eggs first into a separate bowl, and then add them to your larger bowl, to prevent adding a bad egg or egg shells into your batter.

▶ Grease your muffin tin with your favorite fat {even if it's a non-stick pan, trust me!}, or you can use muffin tin liners to make your life a smidge easier.

▶ Fill each muffin section almost to the top. {These only rise a little, so you don't have to worry about them spilling over while cooking.}

▶ Bake for 15–18 minutes, or until the tops have set and they're slightly golden brown.

▶ Allow to cool and enjoy!

Makes: 8–10 muffins

Sweet Potato Broccoli Mix

This is a breakfast that I can totally get behind on a daily basis. It's filling, it's fun, and it spices your week up. The key to having this for breakfast is to either make it on a prep day, or on a day you make a meal with the same ingredients. So if you have a day where you're making roasted sweet potatoes, make extra and then make this the next morning for breakfast! I'm also a huge fan of using a steamfresh bag for the broccoli here to speed up the process of making it. This will also double as a really yummy lunch item, so don't be afraid to mix and match. Want another crazy idea? Make a double batch of this, throw in some cooked chicken, and you could have yourself a really fun dinner recipe!

Ingredients

1 medium sweet potato, cubed and roasted
 {I roasted my sweet potatoes with 1 tsp. cumin
  and ½ tsp. dried rosemary}

olive oil

12 oz. cooked broccoli

6 oz. sausage, cooked and cut into bite-sized pieces

½ small raw onion, finely diced

½ tsp. garlic powder

½ tsp. chili powder

1 tsp. thyme

salt and pepper

2 tsp. apple cider vinegar

How To

▶ If you need to cook your sweet potato, preheat your oven to 400°F.

▶ Cut into cubes, drizzle with olive oil, and sprinkle with cumin and dried rosemary. Then roast for 20–30 minutes, or until the potato is cooked through and golden brown.

▶ Cook your broccoli and sausages separately, using your favorite methods.

▶ Then comes the fun part: add all of your ingredients to a bowl, mix well, and taste test to adjust your seasoning.

▶ Serve it up and dive in!

Serves: 1–2 people

Fancy Scrambled Eggs

So these scrambled eggs aren't fancy-elegant, but they're fancy in the sense that they aren't your typical scrambled eggs. Because these have veggies in them and a little bit of extra fat, they're extremely filling and are going to give you a great big boost of brain power. {Which, let's face it, is exactly what we all need in the morning.} And here's the extra skinny on the serving size: how many people you can serve will depend on if you want leftovers, or if you need to add in an extra egg. For me personally, if I make this with the three eggs and serve it with some kind of meat, I'll have leftovers. If it's just the eggs and no side meat, then the three eggs will fill me up perfectly! Plus, this is perfect to make ahead of time and store in the fridge, only to reheat it when you need to. Feel free to make double or triple the batch to have ready for most of the week!

Ingredients

fat of choice

½ small onion, diced medium-finely

3 button mushrooms, cleaned, de-stemmed, diced medium-finely

½ cup frozen spinach or kale

1 tsp. favorite dried herb {my favorite is dried basil}

½ tsp. garlic powder

salt and pepper

3 large eggs, beaten

Serves: 1–2 people

How To

▶ In a medium skillet, heat your favorite fat over medium heat.

▶ Once your skillet is nice and hot, add in your onions and mushrooms and let them cook for a few minutes.

▶ Add in your spinach or kale, dried herb, garlic powder, salt, and pepper. Let it all cook together until your spinach or kale is heated through and it all looks cooked.

▶ While the vegetables are cooking, crack your eggs into a separate bowl, add a dash of water, and beat them well.

▶ If you use a stainless steel skillet, add a little bit more fat to your pan before adding in your eggs and let it melt in with everything.

▶ Turn your heat down to medium-low and add your eggs.

▶ Scramble the eggs to your liking. When they're almost done, add a tiny bit more fat and turn off the heat. The heat from the pan will finish off the cooking, and the added fat will stop them from overcooking!

▶ Serve however you like and enjoy!

Fritatta

This is a super fun breakfast or dinner item. It combines a frittata and a quiche and it's just all-around yummy. If you're allergic to nuts or you're not a fan of a "crust," then feel free to just add the egg mixture to your pie dish and bake until it's done. And as always, the filling is just an idea. So if you don't have all of the filling ingredients, just use what you have on hand. This is fantastic as leftovers. So if you have the time and ingredients on hand, making two of these at once is never a bad idea!

Ingredients

Crust

½ cup almond flour

1 Tbsp. coconut flour

2 Tbsp. melted coconut oil or butter

1 tsp. Italian seasoning

1 large egg

salt and pepper

extra fat {your butter or coconut oil}

Filling

8 large eggs

1 tsp. each: dried thyme and dried basil

1¼ cups diced cooked chicken

½ medium onion, finely diced

1 cup kale or spinach

½ tsp. garlic powder

½ {12-oz.} bag favorite frozen vegetable mix

salt and pepper

Serves: 2–4 people

How To

▶ Preheat your oven to 375°F.

▶ Mix your crust ingredients together. {It should form a tight, sticky mixture.}

▶ Liberally grease your pie pan {I used a standard-size} with your favorite fat and make sure to grease all the way up the sides.

▶ Dump your crust mix into the pan and evenly spread it out into a single layer. Bring it up the sides of your pie pan if needed {mine went up about ¼ of the way}.

▶ Pop the crust into your oven and bake for 8–10 minutes, or until the dough is firm to the touch but hasn't browned.

▶ While that's baking away, crack all of your eggs into a bowl and beat them slightly. Remember to crack your eggs into a separate bowl before adding them into the larger mixture so you don't accidentally add a bad egg or shells!

▶ Add the rest of your ingredients and mix everything together well.

▶ When your crust is done, add your egg mixture to the pie pan on top of the crust, and place the pan back in the oven.

▶ Bake for 45–60 minutes, or until the eggs are set and the middle is cooked.

▶ Let it cool slightly and then slice and serve!

Lunch

Roasted Garlic Shrimp

I'll be the first to admit that shrimp isn't the cheapest thing to eat. But when you eat it for lunch you can get away with a smaller portion, which makes it the perfect treat for yourself every now and again! The best part is that it's pretty quick to make and is also good at room temperature or even cold. I like to serve this with Zucchini Noodles but it'll also work as is, over cauliflower rice, or even over spaghetti squash.

Ingredients

fat of choice

1 small onion, medium-fine dice

4 button mushrooms, cleaned, de-stemmed and medium-fine dice

1 lb. shrimp, peeled and deveined

1 tsp. dried thyme

½ tsp. garlic powder

1 bulb roasted garlic {around 1–2 Tbsp.} {page 144 in Quick Reference Section}

salt and pepper

Serves: 1–2 people

How To

▶ Heat a medium-sized skillet with your fat of choice on medium heat.

▶ Add in your onion and mushrooms and let them soften.

▶ Once they are ready, add your shrimp, thyme, and garlic powder and mix well.

▶ When your shrimp is almost cooked—you'll know it's cooked when it turns a pretty pink color—add in your roasted garlic, salt, and pepper.

▶ Mix it all around, give it a quick taste, and adjust seasoning if needed.

▶ Serve as is or over Zucchini Noodles and enjoy!

A Quick Note: When buying shrimp, you have many options for how far along it is in the cleaned and cooked process when you buy it. For myself, I think the best deal is generally if you can get it uncooked and de-veined. The de-veining process can take a while, so if all you have to do is pull off the shell, you're good! If you don't really have any time this week, buy the precooked and then just add the shrimp in for the last minute or so of cooking to heat it through.

Lunchtime Spaghetti Squash

Here's a story for you. One day, when I was cooking for this book, I had a whole bunch of leftover spaghetti squash and had no idea what to do with it. Then I said, "Wait, it would make an amazing lunch!" And guess what: it did and it does! This is something I make all the time now because it's so fast and it's so ridiculously good. And if you don't have chicken on hand, don't worry! Just use whatever already cooked meat you have! I actually think this would taste amazing with leftover steak or even chopped up Inside-Out Burgers {page 96}.

Ingredients

1 cup leftover spaghetti squash

1 cup chopped cooked chicken {if you don't have cooked chicken, use any other leftover cooked meat}

about ¼ cup chopped tomatoes

1 tsp. dried basil

1 tsp. garlic powder

juice from half a lemon

salt and pepper

½ batch homemade mayo {page 140 in Quick Reference Section}

chopped raw nuts {optional}

How To

▶ Add all of your ingredients to a bowl, except your mayo, and mix it well.

▶ Add in most of your mayo, mix well, and then add the rest if you need it. {Because spaghetti squash can get soft, it sometimes doesn't need the full amount of mayo. It's better to start with a little and add more if needed.}

▶ Taste test and adjust the seasoning if needed.

▶ Enjoy!

Author's Note: If you don't like mayo or are allergic to eggs, you can drizzle on some olive oil and lemon juice instead. It'll be equally as yummy and filling!

Serves: 1–2 people

Tomato Soup

Apparently Mr. POAB is a huge fan of tomato soup—something I learned when brainstorming the lunch ideas for this book. So I said sure, I can make a super easy, quick one for you. And I did! This literally will take you minutes to make, and I'm sorry in advance if you can't stop at just one bowl. Serve this as is, or use it for a "soup and salad" kind of lunch or dinner. And if you want this to be meaty, add in some diced sausage or cooked chicken.

Ingredients

fat of choice

1 medium onion, diced medium-finely

1 large carrot, peeled and finely diced

½ cup homemade mayo {or coconut milk or heavy cream}

1 {28-oz.} can crushed tomatoes {or fresh crushed tomatoes}

1 cup chicken stock

1 tsp. garlic powder

2 tsp. dried basil

salt and pepper

How To

▶ In a large soup pot, heat up your favorite fat on medium heat.

▶ Add in your onion and carrots and let them soften.

▶ While they're getting all happy in the pot, you can make your mayo if you're going to be using it.

▶ Once your onion and carrots are soft, add in your crushed tomatoes and chicken stock. Give it a good stir.

▶ Add in your mayo {or coconut milk or heavy cream} and your garlic powder, dried basil, and a sprinkle of salt and pepper.

▶ Give everything a big stir and let it simmer for as long as you'd like. It only needs 10–15 minutes!

▶ Serve and enjoy!

Serves: 2–3 people

Chicken Lettuce Wraps

Chicken Lettuce Wraps are pretty much the bomb for lunch. In my mind, there isn't much that's yummier or quicker to make. In the picture on the opposite page, you'll notice that I've got a few different versions of the wrap. There are honestly a million and one different ways to make this, depending on what you have at home when you make them. I personally prefer the "supreme" version that's loaded with veggies, olive oil, and mustard. I also like using the Lemon Lime Chicken {page 115} with this more than any other chicken, because it's already so full of flavor that you can skip the extra seasoning part. In the ingredients list, I listed what I had in the wraps shown, but please, for the love of bacon, don't buy special ingredients. Just use whatever is in the back of your fridge!

And here are a few tips: If you're taking this to work, put your chicken and vegetables in a to-go container and bring yourself a little bit of mustard or olive oil and your lettuce wraps separate. Then you can fill them as you eat them at work without worrying about everything getting messy! Also, you don't have to use romaine lettuce! I use it because it's decently priced and it's easy to eat—but you can use regular lettuce, boston bib, and so on. And lastly, you can totally rock a chicken salad here instead of what I've put together. It doesn't even have to be chicken. You'll see that in one of the meal plans I say a "sausage lettuce wrap," which is just swapping the chicken for sausage.

Ingredients

3–4 leaves romaine lettuce, washed and trimmed if needed

¼–⅓ chicken breast {~½ cup}, diced into bite-sized pieces

favorite veggies, chopped {I used cucumber, tomatoes, and raw onion}

mustard or olive oil {or both!}

salt and pepper

chopped raw nuts {optional}

How To

▶ In your lettuce leaf, place your chicken and any veggies you'd like to add. You don't have to use veggies; you can eat it with chicken only if you want to.

▶ Drizzle on a little bit of olive oil or mustard {or both}. Sprinkle a little bit of salt and pepper and any chopped nuts on top if you'd like!

▶ Enjoy!

Serves: 1 person

Tuna + Roasted Sweet Potato

This is a brain food power-packed lunch. You've got all kinds of fat and proteins mixed with fresh vegetables, making it the perfect way to keep you going all afternoon! This is also a great dinner or bring-to-a-friend's house dish. And if you don't have time to roast up a sweet potato the night before or that morning, you can always quickly bake one in the microwave, chop it up, and add it in! It'll have a slightly different texture, but is still equally as yummy!

If you hate canned tuna or just no tuna in general, don't worry about it: you can sub the tuna out for chicken or turkey instead!

Ingredients

2 {5–6-oz.} cans tuna, fresh cooked tuna, or the same
   amount of cooked chicken

1 avocado, diced

¼ large cucumber, diced

½ small onion, diced

½ large sweet potato, roasted

salt and pepper

1 tsp. dried dill

1 tsp. dried Italian seasoning

1 tsp. mustard

1 batch homemade mayo {page 140
   in Quick Reference Section}

How To

▶ Add all of your ingredients, except your mayo, to a bowl and mix it well.

▶ Add half your batch of mayo in, mix, and then add more mayo if needed.

▶ Taste test and adjust seasoning if needed.

▶ Serve as is or in a lettuce wrap, and enjoy!

Serves: 1–2 people

Burrito Bowl

Favorite. Lunch. Ever. Seriously, this is so easy and has so many different options to it that there's no reason you couldn't make this quickly and whenever you'd like for lunch! The best part is that it utilizes leftovers so you don't have to worry about leftovers going to waste. It's loosely based on a burrito bowl that you might get from a local place for lunch, except that you probably spend at least $8 per burrito bowl when you go out. So why not chop that price tag by a bunch and make yourself a fabulous lunch instead?

Note: I'm going to list the various options within the ingredients list, so all you have to do is pick out what you have on hand the day you make it or when you're planning it out for the week.

Ingredients

~1 cup cauliflower rice, lettuce, white rice, roasted sweet potato, or roasted butternut squash

finely chopped raw onions to taste

chopped tomatoes to taste

1 Inside-Out Burger {page 96} or leftover Taco meat {page 121} to taste

olive oil

fresh lemon juice or your favorite vinegar

salt and pepper

½ tsp. your favorite dried herb {I use oregano}

homemade mayo {optional, see page 140 in Quick Reference Section}

How To

▶ Get your bottom layer of choice {lettuce, white rice, cauliflower rice, roasted sweet potato, or roasted butternut squash} on your plate or in your to-go container.

▶ Add a layer of however much you'd like of both chopped raw onions and chopped tomatoes. If you happen to have some caramelized onions leftover, you could swap those in too. Or try adding a half cup or so of leftover Roasted Veggies.

▶ If you're going to be taking this meal to work with you and you want the meat hot, pack that up in a separate container. Otherwise, chop up your burger and place it on top, or spoon some taco meat on top of your base.

▶ Drizzle with a little bit of olive oil and give it a good spritz of lemon juice {or 2–3 teaspoons of your favorite vinegar}.

▶ Top it all with salt, pepper, and your dried herb. You can stop here and enjoy, or you can add a big spoonful of homemade mayo for some extra nomz!

Serves: 1 person

Dinner + Side Dishes

Spaghetti Squash + Sauce

For the record, I didn't like spaghetti squash until I wrote this book. I know, I know, I'm a little late getting on this bandwagon. When I first went Paleo, I tried making it and it wasn't my favorite, so I just never made it again. Well, long story short, I wanted to step outside my comfort zone a little and I decided to try this little number. And oh my bacon, I'm in love! This was the perfect mix of flavors and textures, and it's so easy. Not to mention the sauce isn't a traditional sauce, because I get bored with normal sauces—I'm sure you do too—so it's just a little fun and creative alternative. If you have a favorite tomato sauce recipe, you can absolutely use it here instead of mine. And don't forget to make extra—leftovers are a meal planner's best friend!

Ingredients

Spaghetti Squash

1 medium spaghetti squash, cut in half, seeds/guts removed

olive oil

salt and pepper

Tomato Sauce

fat of choice

1 medium onion, diced medium-finely

2 carrots, diced medium-finely

2 stalks celery, diced medium-finely

1 lb. ground meat of choice {I prefer beef}

½ {8-oz.} bag frozen pepper strips

½ {16-oz.} bag frozen spinach or kale {or a mix!}

1 Tbsp. each: dried rosemary, dried basil, and Italian seasoning

1 tsp. each: cumin, red hot pepper flakes {optional}, and garlic powder

½ tsp. ground cinnamon

salt and pepper to taste

1 {14-oz.} can diced tomatoes

1 {28-oz.} can crushed tomatoes

2–3 Tbsp. apple cider vinegar

Serves: 2–4 people

How To

▶ Preheat your oven to 375°F.

▶ Rub the inside of each half of the spaghetti squash with olive oil and then sprinkle on salt and pepper. If you'd like, you can also sprinkle on some Italian seasoning or dried basil for extra flavor.

▶ Place on a baking pan cut side–down {so the skin is facing you} and bake for 40–50 minutes, or until the spaghetti squash is easily pierced with a fork.

▶ While it's cooking, you can make your sauce if it hasn't been made yet. If it has been pre-made, just set it on the stove to heat up while the spaghetti squash is cooking.

To Cook the Sauce:

▶ Heat a large pot with your favorite fat {I used grass-fed butter here}.

▶ Add in your onions, carrots, and celery, and let them start to cook. Once they've started to soften, add your ground meat and mix it all together.

▶ Add your spices, herbs, salt, and pepper, and combine again.

▶ Add your diced and crushed tomatoes and apple cider vinegar, and give it a big mix.

▶ Set the heat on low and let it simmer for as long as you can; the longer it sits, the better it'll taste!

▶ Taste test before serving and adjust seasoning as needed.

Vegetable Chili

Here's a little well-kept secret for you: Mr. POAB isn't a fan of chili. I know—crazy, right? For some reason he just doesn't like it… anymore. Apparently he was a huge fan of it back in the day, but since we've been together I've never heard him once say he "enjoys" chili. Well, I, of course, took that as a challenge, and I think I've pretty much nailed it. This time around I made a Vegetable Chili that still has meat in it! It's just super packed with veggies, making it hearty and filling. As always, feel free to add in whatever vegetables you have on hand, or use whatever kinds of meats you have. Don't go out and buy special for this unless you want to. Also, chili is an amazing leftover, so make extra!

Ingredients

fat of choice

1 medium onion, diced medium-finely

½ {12-oz.} pkg. mushrooms, diced medium-finely

2 carrots, peeled and chopped into bite-sized pieces

2 zucchini, washed and chopped into large bite-sized pieces

1 {8-oz.} bag frozen pepper strips

1 {12-oz.} bag frozen mixed vegetables {I used a California blend}

salt and pepper

1 lb. ground beef

2 Tbsp. each: cumin and Italian seasoning

4–5 Tbsp. chili powder {depending on your preference, I used 4 Tbsp.}

1 Tbsp. each: dried basil and dried oregano

2 tsp. garlic powder

1 tsp. red hot pepper flakes {optional}

2–3 Tbsp. apple cider vinegar

1 {28-oz.} can crushed tomatoes

1 {14-oz.} can diced tomatoes

How To

▶ In a large pot {as large as you can go}, heat your favorite fat over medium heat while you chop your veggies.

▶ Add in your vegetables as you chop them, treating this exactly like a "chop and drop." {You chop it and then you drop it into the pot.}

▶ Once the fresh vegetables are in, mix them around and add your frozen veggies. Then sprinkle a little salt and pepper on top.

▶ Add your ground beef and mix well.

▶ Add all your spices, herbs, apple cider vinegar, and some more salt and pepper, and mix well.

▶ Add your two tomato products and mix well again.

▶ Set to a low heat, cover, and let simmer for at least a half hour—the longer it sits, the better.

▶ Serve either as is, or top with your favorite chili toppings {avocado, homemade mayo {page 140}, chopped nuts, guacamole, salsa, and so on}.

▶ Enjoy!

Serves: 2–4 people

Inside-Out Burgers

I'm a huge burger fan. They're pretty much my favorite meal. These Inside-Out Burgers top any other burger I've ever made or had, hands down. They're juicy and flavorful, and the filling in them is kind of a surprise. The best part? You'll more than likely have extra filling, and you've got options on what to do with it. You can be like me and just eat it out of the bowl, you can use it to top your burgers for double goodness, OR you can save it and toss it with some eggs in the morning and use it for breakfast or lunch. See? I told you these burgers were epic! And if you don't have beef on hand or don't like beef, that's totally cool, just use whatever ground meat you have on hand!

Here's a little tip on making sure the filling is usable after you make your burgers: scoop the filling with a tablespoon, plop the filling into your palm {without touching the spoon to your hand}, and don't put the spoon back in the bowl! This way you don't cross contaminate anything and it's still edible!

Ingredients

2 carrots

3–4 slices bacon

½ small onion, diced medium-finely

3 button mushrooms, cleaned, de-stemmed, and diced medium-finely

fat of choice

salt and pepper

1 tsp. dried basil

½ tsp. garlic powder

1–2 tsp. fresh lemon juice

1¼ lb. ground beef

Serves: 2–4 people

How To

► Peel and chop your carrots, put them in a small pot with water, and set them to boil. {You want them tender so they're easily mashed.}

► While the carrots are boiling, dice your bacon and set it in a small skillet to cook. Once it's all crispy, put only the bacon in a small mixing bowl, leaving the fat in your pan.

► Add your diced onion and mushroom to the pan and let cook. While they're cooking, feel free to help yourself to a few pieces of bacon. ;}

► Once cooked, add them to the bowl with your bacon, making sure to add all the fat to the bowl.

► By now your carrots should be good to go, so drain them but keep them in the pot. Add a little bit of your favorite fat, salt, and pepper and mash the carrots. You can use a fork, but I'm really lazy so I use a potato masher to mash it up super quick.

► Add your carrots to your filling bowl and add your basil, garlic powder, lemon juice, and a little more salt and pepper. Mix it all up and give it a quick taste test, adjusting seasoning as needed.

► Now it's time to form your burgers. I like to put my ground meat in a bowl and sprinkle on a little salt and pepper. Mix it lightly. Be careful when dealing with ground meat; don't overmix it, or the meat will become tough and tight!

▶ Form 8–10 equal-sized patties. Half of these are going to have filling, and the other half are going to go on top.

▶ Using a tablespoon measuring spoon, place your filling on half of the formed patties, making sure to keep a clean edge on them for easy sealing.

▶ Place an unused patty on top of one with filling and crimp the sides together. You want to make sure you really pay attention to this part: if you don't pinch the sides together and then smooth it out a little, your burgers could open up when cooking.

▶ Put them in a large skillet over medium-high heat with your favorite fat and cook for 3–6 minutes per a side {or to your level of doneness}. I like to let these rest a few minutes so the juices go back into the meat and the burgers are even tastier.

▶ Serve with your favorite toppings and enjoy!

Liz Special

This is a very "Liz" recipe. It's actually my go-to dinner. It's extremely filling and cheap to make. And if you want to take this from yummy to delicious, try sprinkling on a few dashes of hot sauce or coconut aminos. The flavor you choose will give it a totally different vibe. {Which is perfect because everyone in the family can eat it a different way.} Mr. POAB is a coconut amino's fan—making it more of an "Asian-inspired" dinner—whereas I just like it smothered in hot sauce, because I'm cool like that. If you want to go for the gold, you can also throw on some raw chopped nuts. The options are limitless with this, so go and have fun!

Ingredients

fat of choice

1 lb. ground meat {I like pork}

16-oz. favorite frozen vegetable mix—it's traditional to use the California blend

4–5 large eggs, beaten

2 tsp. favorite dried herb {I used dill}

2 tsp. apple cider vinegar

salt and pepper

How To

▶ Heat a large skillet over medium-high heat with your favorite fat.

▶ Once it's nice and hot, add in your ground meat. Give it a few quick mixes in the pan and then add in your frozen vegetables.

▶ While all of this is cooking, crack your eggs into a bowl, throw in a splash of water, and beat them.

▶ When your meat and veggies are 99% cooked, add your eggs. Give it a few mixes in the pan and then turn off the heat.

▶ Add your herbs, apple cider vinegar, salt, and pepper. Keep mixing until your eggs are cooked. They'll look more creamy than scrambled eggs, which is the amazing part.

▶ Taste test, adjust if needed, and serve up!

Serves: 2–4 people

Zucchini Sticks

I happen to be with a man who is obsessed with all things "breaded." If I could make everything with some form of a Paleo bread coating, he'd be ecstatic. While that's not the best or most practical idea, I decided to make him what is now his new favorite. Mr. POAB will eat this as a snack, with dinner, for dinner, or even for lunch; it's just that good! Here's a really awesome tip for you: if you really love these {like a certain someone we both know}, pre-make a whole bunch of the coating. I'm talking as much as you can—then you can store it in a container and portion it out as you need it. These are also a great way to get your kids in the kitchen and cooking with you!

As a little note: these can flake a little bit once they're cooked, and that's totally normal. If you want them to get crispier, make sure you give them room on the pan—don't overcrowd it—and flip them halfway through cooking.

Ingredients

Zucchini Sticks

2 medium zucchinis
1 large egg, beaten
salt and pepper
½ cup almond flour
2 Tbsp. coconut flour
¼ tsp. garlic powder
1 tsp. Italian seasoning
olive oil

Dipping Sauce

double batch mayo {page 140 in Quick
 Reference Section}
¼ tsp. garlic powder
1 tsp. cumin
juice of half a lemon
salt and pepper

Serves: 2–4 people

{or 1 Mr. POAB}

How to

▶ Preheat your oven to 375°F.

▶ Cut your zucchinis into match sticks and set them aside.

▶ Crack your egg into a small bowl with a small splash of water and a sprinkle of salt and pepper, and then beat it well. Finally, transfer your egg onto a shallow plate with sides.

▶ On a separate plate, add your almond flour, coconut flour, garlic powder, Italian seasoning, salt, and pepper. Mix it all together until combined.

▶ Get a large baking sheet and cover it with aluminum foil. Then drizzle a little bit of olive oil on it and spread the oil out into a thin, even layer.

▶ Now it's time to assemble. Make sure you have everything set up for easy assembly. {I also like to keep one hand for the wet and one hand for the dry, so the batter never creates a really big mess on my hands.}

▶ Coat your zucchini sticks in the egg mixture all the way around, plop them into the almond flour mixture, and coat them evenly but thinly. Remember to tap it against the plate a little to get rid of the excess coating. Place on the pan. Continue on until it's all used up! You might have extra zucchini sticks, which is totally fine and awesome—use those zucchini sticks for lunch tomorrow, or chop them up and use them as a filling for Fancy Scrambled Eggs {page 72} tomorrow morning!

▶ Bake in the oven for 15–25 minutes, until they're cooked through and golden brown.

▶ If you want to make the dip to go with it, make it while your zucchini sticks are cooking.

▶ Serve with your favorite dinner or just dive right in. Enjoy!

Broccoli Salad

This has to be my favorite side dish and it just so happens to be really easy! I normally make it with steamfresh frozen broccoli, so while it's doing it's thing cooking, I'm doing my thing and boom! Quick and easy side dish. Flavor-wise I just adore the combination of broccoli, sausage, onion, and homemade mayo. I have no idea why, but it's beyond yummy and if you decide to chill it, it makes it even better. And you should really try this for lunch, because it's perfect as-is.

Ingredients

12 oz. cooked broccoli florets

6 oz. cooked sausages, in crumbles or bite-sized pieces

1 batch mayo {page 140}

½ medium onion, finely chopped

1 tsp. dried basil

1–2 Tbsp. fresh lemon juice

salt and pepper

slivered or chopped raw nuts {optional}

How To

▶ Cook your broccoli and sausages if you need to, or pop a steamfresh bag of broccoli into the microwave.

▶ While the sausages and broccoli are cooking, make a batch of mayo {page 140}.

▶ To the mayo, add your finely diced onion, broccoli, sausage, basil, lemon juice, salt, and pepper. Mix well.

▶ Add chopped nuts if you'd like. Mix again, taste test, and adjust seasoning as needed.

Author's Note: This side dish is great served either right away at room temperature or served cold. It'll make a stellar side dish to bring to cookouts over the summer!

Serves: 1–3 people

Steak + Eggplant

Steak + Eggplant—now that's what I'm talking about! We've got roasted, we've got tangy, we've got meaty, and we've got yummy, all in one dinner. The best part? You can make bits and pieces of it ahead of time to fit your schedule. The one thing I'll suggest is that if you're not a huge eggplant fan, make sure the eggplant and mushrooms are roasted up fresh. And if you're really anti-eggplant, just swap it out for your favorite vegetable that's along the same lines {like summer squash, zucchini, and so on}. Also, the leftovers are phenomenal, so make extra! And if you don't have enough leftovers for a full lunch, put it over a salad or some cauliflower rice. Now go make this tonight for dinner, and then come back and finish the book.

Ingredients

½ {12-oz.} pkg. mushrooms, cleaned and cut into quarters

¼ large eggplant, cut into large bite-sized pieces

olive oil

dried rosemary

fat of choice

1 medium onion, thinly sliced

1½ lb. your favorite cut of steak, cut into bite-sized pieces

1 tsp. dried thyme

salt and pepper

juice of half a lemon

1 medium tomato, cut into pieces, or ½ pint cherry tomatoes, cut in half

Serves: 2–3 people

How To

▶ Preheat your oven to 400°F.

▶ Cut up your mushrooms and eggplant and lay them in a single layer on a baking pan.

▶ Drizzle a little bit of olive oil on top and sprinkle with rosemary. Mix it slightly with your hands and spread it out again in a single layer.

▶ Roast the vegetables for roughly 20 minutes, or until they're cooked through and smell amazing.

▶ While those are roasting, heat up a large skillet on medium heat with your favorite fat.

▶ Add your onion and let it start to soften and caramelize slightly.

▶ When the onion is pretty much cooked through, add your steak and let it start to cook.

▶ Add your thyme, salt, and pepper, and mix until your steak is cooked to your preferred level of doneness.

▶ When the steak is cooked and your vegetables are cooked, it's time to combine them! Take your pan off the heat, add your Roasted Veggies, and give it a big mix.

▶ Add your lemon juice and tomatoes, give it one more big mix, and then taste test and adjust seasoning as needed!

▶ Enjoy!

Ground Pork + Sweet Potato

One night I made a stir-fry and had a side of baked sweet potato with it. Then me being me, I combined them, added a big spoonful of fat, and mixed it all around. Let me tell you, it was ah-mazing! The best part is that you can bake your sweet potato any way you want. In the oven or in the microwave. Me? I'm lazy and want food ASAP when I cook, so I generally opt for the microwave. You can make this dish any way you want, with any vegetables you have on hand. You just want to make sure it includes meat, baked sweet potato, and lots of your favorite fat. And if you don't like sweet potato, you can substitute it for butternut squash or something equally as yummy!

Ingredients

1 large sweet potato, cooked

fat of choice

1 medium onion, diced medium-finely

1 lb. ground pork

⅓ {16-oz.} bag frozen spinach

12 oz. frozen or cooked green beans

2–3 Tbsp. apple cider vinegar

2 tsp. dried thyme

1 tsp. dried oregano

salt and pepper

How To

▶ If your sweet potato isn't cooked yet, cook it now.

▶ Heat a large skillet on medium heat with your favorite fat.

▶ Add in your onions and let them start to sweat a little bit. When they start to soften, add in your ground pork, spinach, and green beans.

▶ Mix it and let it start to cook.

▶ When it's about halfway cooked, add your apple cider vinegar, thyme, oregano, salt, and pepper, then mix well.

▶ When it's cooked through, add in a big, heaping spoonful or two of your favorite fat and mix well again.

▶ Taste test and adjust seasoning as needed.

▶ Enjoy!

Serves: 2–4 people

Cauliflower Chicken

If we've been friends for a while, you might know that my liking cauliflower is a relatively new thing. Normally it just weirds me out—I mean, come on, it's albino broccoli with a different texture. However, when you roast it, it goes from, "Eh, can barely stand it" to, "Oh my bacon, I can't stop eating this!" Which is why I highly suggest you try this dish if you're anything like me. The coolest part about this dinner? You can use leftover chicken in it, and you can also pre-roast your veggies ahead of time to make your life easier when it comes to putting this together. And don't be afraid to eat this cold—it becomes a "salad" of sorts and goes from dinner to a really cool party dish!

Ingredients

6 medium carrots, washed, peeled, and cut into slightly larger than bite-size pieces

½ large cauliflower head, washed and cut into florets

olive oil

cumin and dried rosemary to taste

fat of choice

1 medium onion, diced medium-finely

½ {12-oz.} pkg. mushrooms, cleaned, de-stemmed and diced

1½ lb. chicken, cut into bite-sized pieces

salt and pepper

½ tsp. garlic powder

1 tsp. dried basil

1 tsp. dried thyme

1–2 Tbsp. apple cider vinegar

1 medium tomato, chopped or half, or 1 pint cherry tomatoes, cut in half

Serves: 2–4 people

How To

▶ Preheat your oven to 400°F.

▶ Prep your carrots and place them on a baking sheet. Drizzle on a little bit of olive oil, then sprinkle on a little bit of cumin and rosemary. Mix it with your hands and then place in the oven.

▶ While the carrots heat up, prep your cauliflower and pull your carrots out of the oven. Place your cauliflower on the baking sheet. Add a little bit more olive oil, cumin, and rosemary, and use a spoon or spatula to toss everything together.

▶ Place it back in the oven and let it roast for 15–20 minutes, or until both vegetables are cooked through.

▶ While they're roasting, start to heat a large skillet on the stove with your favorite fat over medium heat.

▶ Add your onion and mushrooms to the pan and let them start to cook. While they're cooking, if you need to, chop your chicken into bite-sized pieces.

▶ Add the chicken to the pan and allow it to cook through.

▶ Add your remaining ingredients, except for the tomatoes, and mix well. By now your carrots and cauliflower should be roasted, so add them to the pan, along with one more spoonful of your fat of choice, and give it all a big mix.

▶ Turn off the heat, add your chopped tomatoes, and give it all one additional big mix. Give it a quick taste test and adjust the seasoning if needed.

▶ Serve and enjoy!

Butternut Squash Soup

I love soup for dinner! It's comforting, yummy, and filling. I mean seriously, what more could you want in a meal? And then you pair it with a salad and you've got the best meal ever. This soup in particular is my new favorite. I've always liked the idea of a butternut squash soup, but because Mr. POAB has a firm dislike of all soups that are puréed, super smooth, and without texture, I've always refrained from making it. Then it hit me, I can make this soup and make the both of us happy. Plus, I wouldn't have to worry about using all sorts of fancy gadgets to get it to where it should be texture-wise.

However, if you're in love with all soups that are super smooth and puréed, go to town on it. One thing to note is that this ends up texture-wise more like a chowder. Which apparently makes it amazing {according to a certain someone}, but if you want it to be more soup-like, feel free to add some more chicken stock. I personally like it a little bit thinner, so I just add a little bit extra to my bowl and mix it around. Which means this soup is super easy to customize. I know, I know, it's the best soup ever.

And if you don't have sausages on hand or you don't want to use them, you can totally add chicken, turkey, ham, or some kind of small meatball to this instead. Just use whatever you have on hand!

Ingredients

1 medium butternut squash {mine was 2¾ lb.}, peeled and cubed

water

1 medium onion, caramelized {~¼ cup}

fat of choice

salt and pepper

1 Tbsp. Italian seasoning {or your favorite dried herb}

8 oz. sausage, cut into bite-sized pieces

3–4 cups chicken stock {depending on how thin you like your soup}

Serves: 2–4 people

How To

▶ In a large pot {large enough to make soup in} add in your cubed butternut squash and cover it with water. Turn on the heat and allow to boil until it's tender.

▶ While that's boiling away, caramelize your onion.

▶ Drain the butternut squash and keep it in the pot. Add in your caramelized onion, fat of choice to taste, and your salt, pepper, and dried herb. Then use a potato masher and smash away. I like to smash it to the point where it's almost "smooth" but still has a few chunks in it to give it texture. But you can mash it to whatever texture makes you happy.

▶ Add your sausages and chicken stock and let simmer for at least 10 minutes.

Quick Tip: If you're going to let the soup simmer for a while, then you can add uncooked sausages and let it cook in the soup. If you need this to be done ASAP, just precook your sausage.

▶ Taste test and adjust the seasoning as needed.

▶ Serve and enjoy!

Chicken, Lemon, + Broccoli

Chicken and broccoli is a fun dinner. It's creamy, it's citrusy, it's tangy: pretty much everything you want in a dinner. The nice thing is that you can use any type of cooked chicken and broccoli you like. You can use leftover chicken from a few nights ago, chicken from making chicken stock, or you can cook it fresh that night; whatever you have on hand works. The same goes for the broccoli: you can steam it yourself, roast it, use a steamfresh microwaveable bag {which is my favorite because it makes dinner that much quicker}, frozen, and so on.

Ingredients

fat of choice

1 medium onion, diced medium-finely

½ {12-oz.} pkg. mushrooms, cleaned, de-stemmed, and sliced

1½–2 lb. chicken, chopped into bite-sized pieces

1 tsp. cumin

1–2 lemons

12 oz. cooked broccoli

1 tsp. dried basil

1 tsp. dried oregano

salt and pepper

How To

▶ Heat a large skillet with your fat of choice over medium heat.

▶ Add your onion and mushrooms and let them start to soften.

▶ While they are cooking, chop up your chicken and add it to the skillet. Mix well and allow it to cook.

▶ When it's almost cooked through, add in your cumin, juice of half a lemon, and your broccoli. Mix well.

▶ Add your basil, oregano, and juice of another half a lemon to the pan. Add a little more fat, salt, and pepper to the pan when your chicken is cooked. Mix it once again.

▶ Taste test and adjust seasoning as needed. Depending on how juicy your lemon is, you might need another half or whole lemon's worth of juice.

▶ Enjoy!

Serves: 2–4 people

Lemon Lime Chicken

This recipe is inspired by my dad. He makes his own version of Lemon Lime Chicken that's pretty amazing. I wanted to remake it so it had a little brighter flavor and would work well with other dishes. The seasoning blend for this can be made in advance and can even be premade in a large batch and stored to use whenever you're ready. You can even use this as a premixed herb blend for any chicken or fish dish that you want.

Ingredients

3 lemons, 2 sliced and 1 juiced

4 limes, 2 sliced and 2 juiced

1 tsp. garlic powder

2 Tbsp. dried dill

1 Tbsp. each: Italian seasoning and dried oregano

4–6 boneless, skinless chicken breasts {2½–3 lb.}

salt and pepper

Serves: 2–4 people

How To

▶ Preheat your oven to 375°F.

▶ Slice and juice your lemons and limes into a small bowl. Place the slices of lemons and limes in the bottom of your baking dish.

▶ In another small bowl, mix your garlic powder, dried dill, Italian seasoning, and dried oregano.

▶ Rinse and pat your chicken dry, leaving them bottoms up.

▶ Sprinkle salt and pepper on the chicken and then liberally sprinkle on the herb blend.

▶ Place the chicken breasts in your baking dish {on top of your lemon and lime slices} right-side up {the side that isn't seasoned}.

▶ Sprinkle on more salt and pepper, and then pour your lemon-lime juice over all the chicken.

▶ Sprinkle on more of the herb blend.

▶ Pour in a little bit of water to the bottom of the pan so it comes up about ½–¾ inch from the bottom.

▶ Bake in the oven for 35–50 minutes. {Really, it depends on how much chicken and how thick it is.} You want to cook it until the juices run clear, it's not pink inside and is cooked to 165°F.

▶ I like to baste my chicken a few times while it's cooking—mainly when I'm just checking in to see if it's done. I do this about 3–4 times. Then baste it one more time when it comes out of the oven and let it rest for just a few minutes so it absorbs all the juice.

▶ Serve and enjoy! :}

Rosemary Lime Pork Chops

Pork chops are kind of cool. I don't eat them very often because I never know what to do with them. Then one day I was just chilling in the kitchen and saw a whole bunch of limes sitting there and boom, instant pork chop recipe idea! And not to toot my own horn, but this recipe is pretty great. It combines vegetables, meat, tang, and a little bit of "ohhh, what is that? It's wicked good!" all in one dinner! It's best served with either spaghetti squash, cauliflower rice, or white rice.

Ingredients

fat of choice

4 boneless, skinless pork chops {about 1–1½ lb.}

salt and pepper

dried rosemary

1 medium onion, thinly sliced

½ {12-oz.} pkg. mushrooms, cleaned, de-stemmed, and chopped

1 {8-oz.} bag frozen pepper strips

1 {14-oz.} can diced tomatoes, drained

1 tsp. garlic powder

1 tsp. dried oregano

2 tsp. cumin

juice from 2–3 limes

Serves: 2–4 people

How To

▶ Heat a large skillet on medium-high heat with your fat of choice.

▶ On one side of your pork chops, sprinkle some salt, pepper, and a liberal sprinkle of rosemary. By now your fat should be nice and hot, so place your pork chop seasoning-side down in the pan.

▶ While it's starting to sear, sprinkle the other side with your salt, pepper, and liberal sprinkle of rosemary. After a few minutes {roughly 3–5} flip your pork chop over and let it sear on the other side. While they're searing, I like to chop up my onions and my mushrooms.

▶ When the pork chops are seared on both sides, pull them out of the pan, place them on a dish, and set it aside.

▶ Put a little bit more fat in your skillet and add your onions and mushrooms. Let them cook for a few minutes, and then add the rest of your ingredients, including another sprinkle of salt and pepper. The amount of lime juice you put in will depend on how juicy your limes are and how big of a lime fan you are.

▶ Give everything a big mix, nestle your pork chops into the pan {make sure you add any drippings or juice into the pan as well}, and cover.

▶ Allow everything to cook for 15–20 minutes on a medium-low heat, or until your pork chops are cooked all the way through. You can pull your pork chops out and then give the rest of it a quick taste test and adjust the seasoning as needed.

▶ Serve and enjoy!

Blueberry Chicken Salad

This dish makes me ridiculously happy. I think it might be because the whole thing turns purple from the blueberries, which totally makes me feel like a kid! But the dish itself is so good. I love, love, love the combination of tangy, meaty, and slightly sweet. Plus, the ingredients are all things you generally have at home, meaning it is inexpensive to make. This is also a great meal to make a day or two ahead of time if you can, so plan to eat this on your busiest night of the week in order to make your life a little easier. And yes, you read the ingredient list right; I went with frozen blueberries on this one.

Also, I love serving this with roasted sweet potatoes or vegetables. Something about the cold and hot combination makes me even happier {if that's possible} than the chicken salad already does.

Ingredients

½ medium onion, finely diced

1 bell pepper, washed and roughly diced

½ large cucumber, washed and roughly diced

2–3 cups cooked, diced chicken {depending on how much chicken you like}

1 cup frozen blueberries

1 Tbsp. dried dill

1 tsp. dried thyme

salt and pepper

1–2 Tbsp. apple cider vinegar

1 batch mayo {page 140 in Quick Reference section}

How To

▶ Chop up your fresh vegetables and add them into a large bowl.

▶ Add in your chicken, blueberries, herbs, salt, pepper, and apple cider vinegar, then mix.

▶ Add in half the mayo and give it a great big stir. At this point, see if you need more mayo and add in just enough to make it to your liking!

▶ Taste test and adjust the seasoning as needed.

▶ Eat as is or serve with your favorite side dish, and enjoy!

Serves: 2–3 people

Tacos

Tacos, how I've had a love-hate relationship with you for most of my life! As a kid, "taco night" was never my favorite. {Mainly because I didn't like my topping options and I wasn't a fan of tortilla wraps.} But never fear, I have finally created the prettiest, yummiest taco recipe ever. It's easy, it's delicious, and it can be served a million and one different ways. Plus it rocks as leftovers. Not to mention that you can always use leftover taco meat as the meat for a tomato sauce. You can also toss it in a chili or use it for the Burrito Bowls {page 89}! Which means making extra is more than encouraged.

Ingredients

fat of choice

1 medium onion, diced medium-finely

½ {12-oz.} pkg. mushrooms, cleaned, de-stemmed, and sliced

1 lb. ground beef

2 Tbsp. chili powder

1 Tbsp. cumin

2 tsp. dried basil

1 tsp. garlic powder

2 tsp. dried oregano

2 Tbsp. apple cider vinegar

1 {14-oz.} can diced tomatoes, drained

salt and pepper

Serves: 2–3 people

How To

▶ In a skillet, heat your favorite fat on medium-high heat.

▶ Add in your onion and mushrooms and let them start to cook.

▶ After a few minutes, once the onions become soft, add your ground beef and mix.

▶ When your beef is about half cooked, add in all of your spices and herbs, and then mix well. You want the herbs and spices to warm up just a little before you add the rest of the ingredients.

▶ Add your apple cider vinegar, tomatoes, salt, and pepper. Mix well and allow everything to finish cooking.

▶ Because these are tacos, the longer the mixture sits, the better. So you can either serve right when the beef is done, or you can let it sit on the stove on low, covered for a few hours.

▶ Serve these with lettuce wraps, as is, or over your favorite "noodle" for something different. Don't forget to include your favorite toppings if desired {avocados, nuts, homemade mayo, shredded raw cheese, and so on}.

Roasted Veggies

I happen to be one of those people who can eat roasted veggies like some people eat candy. I just can't stop, they're so good! Which is why you needed this recipe—it's just that good. This pairs amazingly well with pretty much everything, but especially Lemon Lime Chicken {page 115} and Inside-Out Burgers {page 96}. You can also make a double or triple batch of these and use the leftovers for lunch or to toss into a chili, soup, or stir-fry throughout the week!

Ingredients

2 medium zucchini, cut into large chunks

½ {12-oz.} pkg. mushrooms, de-stemmed, cleaned, and cut into quarters

4–6 carrots, cut into medium-sized pieces

olive oil

salt and pepper

1 tsp. each: dried rosemary and cumin

½ tsp. garlic powder

½ fresh lemon {optional}

How To

▶ Preheat your oven to 375°F.

▶ Wash and chop your vegetables and add them to a large baking pan. Try to keep your zucchini and carrots similar sized, but I always like to make the carrot pieces a little bit smaller as they take the longest to roast up!

▶ Drizzle your olive oil on top of the veggies, and sprinkle your salt and pepper, rosemary, cumin, and garlic powder on top.

▶ Use your hands to mix it all together and then pop into the oven for 40–45 minutes, or until your veggies are roasted and smell amazing!

▶ Spritz on a little bit of fresh lemon juice when they come out of the oven for an added layer of flavor!

▶ Serve and enjoy! :}

Serves: 2–3 people

Vegetable Chicken Soup

If we've been friends for a while, you'll know that I have a mild obsession with chicken soup. It's my favorite—I think it can make any day go from craptastic to amazing. This version of chicken soup is pretty much my ultimate favorite. It's a mix of vegetable and chicken soup, so you're literally going to make everyone happy. Not to mention that this is wicked filling. One bowl of this, and I'm pretty much good. If you want to make this even fancier, you can put cauliflower rice or white rice at the bottom of your bowl {just a few spoonfuls} and it then takes this soup to an entirely new level of epic. If you decide to not make your own stock, make sure you read the ingredients of the stock you do buy, because a lot of times they can slip gluten, wheat, and soy into store-bought stocks! And go for the low sodium—because overly salty chicken soup isn't anyone's idea of a good time!

Ingredients

fat of choice

1 medium onion, diced medium-finely

3 carrots, diced medium-finely

2 stalks of celery, diced medium-finely

½ {12-oz.} pkg. mushrooms, cleaned, de-stemmed, and diced

¼ large butternut squash, peeled and cut into bite-sized pieces

1 large zucchini, cut into bite-sized pieces

at least 3 cups cooked chicken

2 tsp. apple cider vinegar

2 tsp. each: dried basil and dried thyme

salt and pepper

6–9 cups chicken stock {page 141}

How To

▶ Place a soup pot on medium heat and add your favorite fat.

▶ Add your onion, carrots, celery, and mushrooms. While they're cooking away, peel and dice your butternut squash. Add it to the pot and give it a big mix.

▶ Wash, chop, and add your zucchini as well. Then add your cooked chicken. I measured mine at about 3 cups, but if you want to add more I always say go for it! Just make sure you'll still have leftovers for other recipes if you need it.

▶ Add your apple cider vinegar, dried basil, thyme, and salt and pepper. Go easy on the salt, because the stock already has great flavor and might not need it!

▶ Start with adding somewhere around 6 cups of chicken stock. If you like a thinner soup add more; but if not, just keep it where it is!

▶ Let it simmer for at least a half hour, taste test, and adjust your seasonings as need.

▶ Serve and enjoy!

Serves: 2–3 people

Fish Cakes

Let's be honest for a moment. I was never a fish cake fan as a kid, because the smell of the salted cod being soaked was pretty pungent and, well, gross to my younger self. So I've stayed away from these my whole life. And then I became a food blogger and decided to write a book, and needed a fish recipe, so I thought I'd try to tackle this. Well, color me impressed, because these Fish Cakes are pretty much the best thing ever. They're an awesome mix of creamy and crunchy, and are jam-packed full of flavor. Not to mention they're easy!

Ingredients

1 lb. mild white fish, like halibut or cod

salt and pepper

½ small onion, finely diced

2 button mushrooms, cleaned, de-stemmed, and finely diced

1 tsp. garlic powder

½ tsp. cumin

1 tsp. dried thyme

1 tsp. dried basil

juice of half a fresh lemon

1 Tbsp. coconut flour

2 eggs

fat of choice

Serves: 2–3 people

How To

▶ Preheat your oven to 350°F.

▶ Rinse your fish under cool water and pat dry. Run your fingers up and down the fish, pressing lightly to check for bones. If you find any, just pull them out!

▶ Place your fish in a baking dish and sprinkle on a little bit of pepper and a tiny, tiny amount of salt.

▶ Bake in the oven until the fish is cooked to your liking {around 15–20 minutes}.

▶ While your fish is cooking, combine the rest of your ingredients in a mixing bowl.

▶ When the fish is done, let it cool for just a few minutes and then flake it with a fork. Add it to the bowl with the rest of the ingredients and mix well. I like to mix this with my hands at this point, but you can absolutely use a fork instead.

▶ Form your Fish Cakes into whatever size you'd like—I make mine somewhere in-between a golf ball and a tennis ball size. It's best if you can make them all at once and then cook them—that way you ensure even cooking on all of them!

▶ Heat a large skillet over medium-high heat with your favorite fat—and don't be skimpy!

▶ Place your Fish Cakes in the pan once it's heated, and allow them to cook on one side. Remember not to overcrowd your pan; cook these in batches if you have to! When the Fish Cakes starts to look golden brown on the bottom edge and on the bottom {around 5 minutes}, you can gently flip them over and cook the other side.

▶ When they're done, serve them with your favorite side dish and an extra spritz of lemon if you'd like!

Eggplant Stackers

I'm not too sure if dinner could get much easier than this. But it's not just easy to make, it's also fun to eat. You don't even have to serve these pre-stacked. Just leave the components on the table and let everyone make their own! Which will totally make your life easier! The coolest part? You don't even have to use tomato sauce. You could get wild and crazy and use a fresh salsa, leftover chili, some kind of chutney, or even leftover stir-fry! I know, I know, this beyond awesome, right? Here's the one catch—if you're a fickle eggplant eater, you need to make sure you roast your eggplant right before you eat it. If you'll eat eggplant all day everyday, you can probably get away with pre-roasting, it just might have a softer texture! Now let's go on to this oh-so-pretty recipe, shall we?

Ingredients

1 eggplant, cut into ¼-inch disks

olive oil

salt and pepper

Italian seasoning to taste

1 large onion, caramelized

5–10 oz. sausage {depending on how many you're making}

1–2 cups tomato sauce {use leftover sauce like the one from the Spaghetti Squash + Sauce on page 93}

Serves: 2–3 people

How To

▶ Preheat your oven to 400°F.

▶ Cut your eggplants into pretty disks and then lay them on a aluminum foil baking sheet. {The aluminum foil is optional; it just makes for easy clean up and ensures nothing sticks!}

▶ Brush on a little bit of olive oil—it's easier to put it on your hand and rub it onto the eggplant, or use a pastry brush. Otherwise you run the risk of putting too much olive oil on without even realizing it because of how absorbent eggplant is!

▶ Sprinkle on a little bit of Italian seasoning, salt, and pepper. Flip the eggplant disks over and repeat.

▶ Place in oven and bake for 20–30 minutes, or until the eggplant looks really pretty and roasted/cooked through.

▶ While it's roasting, reheat your tomato sauce and, if you need to, cook up your onions and sausage.

▶ When the eggplant is roasted and everything is heated, stack up your eggplants! Start with a layer of eggplant, and then add sauce, sausage, onion, and continue on for two to three stacks.

▶ Serve with your favorite side dish and enjoy!

Desserts + Snacks

Raspberry Mug Cake

Oh, I went there—what's a cookbook without a few treat recipes, right? And this one literally takes minutes to make. I'm one of those people who sometimes wants a dessert, but I don't want to spend the 10 minutes putting the batter together and then the eight-to-forever minutes it takes to actually cook it. I mean, come on, that's just not happening on a Thursday night. So I give you the mug cake! This mug cake has raspberries in it, but you can use whatever you want. I've made one with blueberries, I've made them plain, some people have told me they've added shredded coconut. Your imagination is the limit on this dessert! Just as a note—I normally use a regular coffee mug and it fills it up about halfway {for the photo I made a double batch!}! So what are you waiting for? Go make this and get back here and finish the book!

Ingredients

1 large egg, beaten

1 Tbsp. almond flour

1 Tbsp. coconut flour

2 Tbsp. chocolate chips

1 tsp. vanilla extract

2 Tbsp. maple syrup

1–2 Tbsp. frozen raspberries

Serves: 1 person

How To

► In a microwave-safe mug, add your egg and beat it well.

► Add your coconut and almond flour and mix well with a fork.

► Add the rest of your ingredients. When it comes to the frozen raspberries, just use your fingers to break them up and mix well.

► Cook in the microwave for 1½–2 minutes, or until everything is set. It might still look a little "wet" on top, but that's totally fine—it's just from the frozen raspberries!

► If you can let it cool a little, it's a good idea. But if not, you can be like me and dive right in!

► Enjoy!

Author's Note: Make sure your chocolate is dairy, soy, and nut free if possible—but the soy free is a must! My favorite brand is the Enjoy Life Chocolate Chips! And if you can't find chocolate chips, you can always cut up your favorite dark chocolate bar into little pieces and add it in!

If you don't have a microwave, you can always try putting it in the oven at 350°F until the center is set/cooked. {It'll probably take 4–8 minutes—just keep an eye on it!}

Faux Deviled Eggs

I love a good deviled egg, but let's be real—they can take forever to make. You have to scoop out the yolk, make the mayo, make the filling, re-stuff, and so on, and so forth. And there is no way that you've got time for that if you're trying to grab a quick snack or add something a little extra to your lunch this week. So my solution? A Faux Deviled Egg, of course! They're called "faux" for a reason—they give you the feeling of a deviled egg without the steps you read above! And the toppings are just ideas; you can get as crazy as you want with these. My favorite was the scallions on top, but it'll come as no surprise to know that Mr. POAB's favorite was the bacon-topped one!

When you're making the toppings for these, either chop or cook them along with your prep day, or whatever you're doing the night before that morning. So, for instance, if you're having bacon with breakfast, just cook up an extra slice, store it in the fridge, and boom! It's ready to assemble whenever you are!

Ingredients

1–2 hard-boiled eggs, sliced in half lengthwise

salt and pepper

Topping Ideas

bacon

scallions

mustard

cumin

finely diced tomatoes {I quartered cherry tomatoes}

How To

▶ Slice your egg in half, give it a tiny sprinkle of salt and pepper, and then go to town with the toppings!

If you're looking for something really quick and easy, the mustard and cumin topping is my favorite. It's really good served up with some cold chicken, and boom—2 minute lunch!

The finely diced tomatoes version can be taken a step further by sprinkling on your favorite herb or even topping it with a little super finely-diced red onion!

As you can see, this is pretty limitless and can also make a really fun, easy appetizer at a party! So go make yourself some hard-boiled eggs and experiment with your favorite topping combinations!

Serves: 1 person

Maple Bacon Cookies

Yes, I put bacon in a cookie—you're welcome! If you're already a lover of all things bacon and cookie related, this recipe is going to be a hit. If, however, you're like one of my friends, you're giving me this look of "ummm… next!" don't turn that page! Keep reading, and make these just once! I promise you, they're going to be the best cookie you've ever eaten! They're almost like a thin, soft sugar cookie—with bacon.

And before we dive into the recipe, I just want to let you know that this batter is thin. When you put it on the cookie sheet, it might spread out to be super, super thin. That's totally fine—the cookies will still be amazing, but they will have a tendency to break a bit easier and crumble a little. The best way to avoid that is to make sure your bacon fat has cooled down. You still want it a liquid, but you want it to be cool so it doesn't thin out the batter. If you end up putting the bacon fat in too hot and the batter is too thin for you, you can put it in the fridge for 5–10 minutes, or until it firms up just a tad! All right, let's make some cookies!

Ingredients

1 cup blanched almond flour

2 large eggs

2–3 Tbsp. bacon fat

1 Tbsp. vanilla extract

3 Tbsp. good-quality maple syrup {either grade B or Dark Amber Grade A}

4 slices bacon

Makes: 10 cookies

How To

▶ Preheat your oven to 350°F.

▶ Combine all of your ingredients except your bacon and mix well. Don't forget to crack your eggs in a separate bowl first to ensure you don't get a bad egg or any shells in your batter!

▶ Chop your bacon into rough, big pieces and add them to the batter. Mix well again.

▶ Line a baking sheet with either parchment paper or aluminum foil and get yourself a teaspoon measuring spoon.

▶ Measure out 1 heaping teaspoon of batter per a cookie. These guys do spread out in the oven a little bit, so make sure to give them some room!

▶ Cook them for 8–10 minutes, or until the edges are golden brown.

▶ Let them cool down and then use a spatula to get them off the cookie sheet. Serve and enjoy!

Quick Reference

The recipes in this section are ones you've probably already seen on the website, or in my first book, *Paleo on a Budget*, but I felt like they needed to be here for easy, quick access. That way you don't have to go searching through a million different spots to find out how to do it! Hence the "Quick Reference" title of the section! You'll find all the important basics, like how to make chicken stock and roast different foods, and how to make mayo! Enjoy!

Mayo

There is no exact amount that this recipe will serve, because it depends on your egg yolk size and how thick you like your mayo.

❖❖❖ Ingredients

1 large egg yolk

extra-light olive oil*

lemon juice or apple cider vinegar

salt and pepper

* I can't give you an exact measurement for how much olive oil to use—every egg yolk, kitchen, person, pouring speed, phase of the moon, and so on, makes it an "as much as you need" situation. I will say you'll go through at least ½ cup of olive oil.

❖❖❖

Serving size varies

How To

▶ In a small bowl {not the one you're making your mayo in}, crack your egg and gently scoop out the yolk with your hand. You want to do this to ensure you're only getting egg yolk and not too much, if any, egg white into the mayo.

▶ Place the egg yolk in a medium bowl. Give it a good whisk to break it up. Then, slowly—let me repeat—slowly. So slowly it hurts, add some olive oil while whisking. Don't add olive oil without whisking. It's crucial to make sure the emulsion takes place almost instantly. {After you've become a mayo pro, you'll be able to tell almost instantly if your emulsion took!}

▶ Occasionally, I'll take a break from adding in olive oil and just give it a really good whisk to ensure it's nice and happy.

▶ You'll know it's done when the majority of your mayo is a ball on your whisk {you'll be able to literally pick up your whisk, hold it upright, and your mayo will stay put}.

▶ At this point, pat yourself on the back—you've made mayo!

▶ Now here comes the flavoring part. Add in about a teaspoon of either lemon juice or apple cider vinegar. Me personally? I like adding in lemon juice, but apple cider vinegar is cheaper—so go with whatever you have on hand right now.

▶ Mix, add in a little salt and pepper, and stir. Taste test and add extra of whatever is needed.

Chicken Stock

Makes: around 8–10 cups chicken stock, and at least 5–6 cups cooked chicken meat. It will vary from chicken to chicken.

Ingredients

1 whole chicken {about 4–5 lb.}

2 medium onions, cut into quarters

3 carrots, cut into thirds

3 stalks celery

oregano, parsley, and salt and pepper to taste

1 splash apple cider vinegar

11–12 cups water

How To

▶ Rinse off your chicken and put it in a big soup pot. Make sure you take out giblets/neck if it's included. You can add it to the stock if you like, but that's optional!

▶ This is where it gets easy. Just chop your onions in quarters. No need to peel them, just use them as is. Cut the carrots and celery in half, rinse, and add it in {again, no peeling needed at all}.

▶ Add a big pinch of both parsley and oregano {around a tablespoon each}, and then add your salt. Don't skimp on salt—if you do, it'll end up tasting a little off. You want to add at least a tablespoon, and after you make your first batch, you'll know how you'd like to adjust it if you need to!

▶ Top with water. Your water should come up about an inch above your chicken. Turn your stove on high heat.

▶ Bring your stock to a boil, and then reduce the heat to low and simmer for about 3–3½ hours, uncovered. If you start to get really low on liquid, feel free to top with some more water.

▶ When it's done, pull out the chicken and place it into a large bowl. Get a big bowl and a strainer and strain the stock into the bowl. Set aside.

▶ Shred all the chicken meat with your fingers {or two forks} and put it into a separate bowl. Store it in the fridge or use it for dinner. Throw out your remaining used veggies. Either throw out the carcass, or save it and use it to make bone broth.

▶ When the stock is room temperature, cover and put it in fridge, or use it immediately for a soup {or just drink a mug of it!}.

▶ Enjoy!

Authors' Note: If you can't afford a whole chicken or if you can't find one, you can use large pieces of chicken with the bone in. Just make sure you get 4–5 pounds of it!

Stir-Fry 101

Ingredients

fat of choice

fresh vegetables, or 1 {8–12-oz.} bag frozen vegetables

1 lb. ground meat or chopped chicken

salt and pepper

~1 Tbsp. favorite herbs, spices, or a mix

optional: apple cider vinegar, lemon juice, hot sauce, chopped raw nuts, and so on.

Serves: 2–4 people

How To

▶ Get a large skillet heating on medium-high heat with your fat of choice. Add in your favorite vegetables.

▶ After it's started to cook, add in your meat and let it cook.

▶ When it's halfway done, add your seasonings, salt, and pepper and anything else you want.

▶ Let it finish cooking. Taste test and adjust the seasonings if need.

Zucchini Noodles

Ingredients

1 zucchini, washed

Serves: 1–2 people

How To

▶ Wash your zucchini and chop off the ends.

▶ Use a peeler to peel the top layer of green skin off of your zucchini and discard the peel.

▶ Use your peeler again to make the "noodles." I like to peel one side, turn the zucchini to a new side, peel again, and continue. This is to ensure that you're using the zucchini evenly and are getting the most noodles out of it.

▶ Once you hit the core and can see seeds, stop. But wait — don't toss the core! Save it and freeze it to add to your next batch of vegetable or chicken stock.

▶ Now you can serve your Zucchini Noodles, or store them in the fridge for later!

▶ Enjoy. :)

How to Boil an Egg

⚙⚙⚙

Ingredients

eggs, any size, and as many as you'd like to fit into the pot

⚙⚙⚙

Serving size varies

How To

▶ Place your eggs in a pot with cold water, making sure the water sits about an inch or two over the eggs.

▶ Leave the pot uncovered, set it to high heat, and allow it to come to a boil. Once it reaches a boil, turn off the heat and cover your pot.

▶ Allow it to sit on the stove, covered, for 10 minutes.

▶ When it's done, drain the water from the pot, leaving the eggs inside, and carefully give the pot a good shake so the eggs hit the side and it starts to break up the shells a bit.

▶ I like to refill the pot with cold water again and then drain and shake two to three times, but that's totally personal preference!

▶ Place the eggs in a bowl of cold water.

▶ To remove the shells: place some paper towels down on your counter and roll the egg around to break up the shell further. Then peel the shell off. Place the eggs back in the cold water.

▶ Continue until all the eggs are peeled, and place them in a storage container. Store in the fridge.

Roasting Veggies + Garlic

Vegetables

Ingredients

your favorite vegetables {carrots, onions, mushrooms, parsnips, and so on}
olive oil
salt and pepper
herb{s} of choice {optional}

How To

▶ Preheat your oven to 375°F.

▶ Wash your vegetables and peel if necessary. Cut them all into similar-sized pieces for even cooking, and place them on your baking sheet. You want to make sure you pick vegetables that roast for roughly the same time if you are using one baking sheet. For instance, I wouldn't roast cherry tomatoes and carrots on the same tray, because the tomatoes will finish first!

▶ Drizzle some olive oil on top of your vegetables and sprinkle them with salt, pepper, and herbs if you're using them. Toss together gently with your hands and spread the vegetables into a single layer.

▶ Roast for 20–30 minutes, or until everything is cooked through and has that beautiful "roasted" look! It's ideal to flip them over halfway through cooking, but if you forget, don't stress about it!

Garlic

Makes: 1 bulb of garlic

Ingredients

1 garlic bulb
olive oil
herbs {optional}

How To

▶ Preheat your oven to 400°F.

▶ Cut the top off the garlic bulb, about an eighth to a quarter of the way down.

▶ Place the garlic on a medium-sized piece of aluminum foil. Then drizzle a little bit of olive oil on it and rub it over the top. At this point, if you'd like to, you can sprinkle a little bit of your favorite herbs on top.

▶ Bring up the sides of the aluminum foil and cover the bulb tightly.

▶ Place on a baking sheet and roast for at least 30–40 minutes, or until caramelized. The best way to tell if it's done is to squeeze the sides of the garlic {while in the foil}. If you can squeeze it easily, it's done. {When doing this, make sure you use a dish towel or something when touching the sides so you don't burn yourself!}

▶ When the garlic is done cooking, allow it to cool, remove from the foil, and eat up!

Cooking Measurement Equivalents

Cups	Tablespoons	Fluid Ounces
⅛ cup	2 Tbsp.	1 fl. oz.
¼ cup	4 Tbsp.	2 fl. oz.
⅓ cup	5 Tbsp. + 1 tsp.	
½ cup	8 Tbsp.	4 fl. oz.
⅔ cup	10 Tbsp. + 2 tsp.	
¾ cup	12 Tbsp.	6 fl. oz.
1 cup	16 Tbsp.	8 fl. oz.

Cups	Fluid Ounces	Pints/Quarts/Gallons
1 cup	8 fl. oz.	½ pint
2 cups	16 fl. oz.	1 pint = ½ quart
3 cups	24 fl. oz.	1½ pints
4 cups	32 fl. oz.	2 pints = 1 quart
8 cups	64 fl. oz.	2 quarts = ½ gallon
16 cups	128 fl. oz.	4 quarts = 1 gallon

Other Helpful Equivalents

1 Tbsp.	3 tsp.
8 oz.	½ lb.
16 oz.	1 lb.

Metric Measurement Equivalents

Approximate Weight Equivalents

Ounces	Pounds	Grams
4 oz.	¼ lb.	113 g
5 oz.		142 g
6 oz.		170 g
8 oz.	½ lb.	227 g
9 oz.		255 g
12 oz.	¾ lb.	340 g
16 oz.	1 lb.	454 g

Approximate Volume Equivalents

Cups	US Fluid Ounces	Milliliters
⅛ cup	1 fl. oz.	30 ml
¼ cup	2 fl. oz.	59 ml
½ cup	4 fl. oz.	118 ml
¾ cup	6 fl. oz.	177 ml
1 cup	8 fl. oz.	237 ml

Other Helpful Equivalents

½ tsp.	2½ ml
1 tsp.	5 ml
1 Tbsp.	15 ml

Recipe Index

About the Author

ELIZABETH MCGAW is convinced she was born with a camera in one hand and a chef's knife in the other. She attributes her love of cooking to her father, who taught her everything she knows about preparing a meal. As for her love of photography, she attributes that to the old Polaroid camera she received as a child. Armed with both passions, she created a blog called *Paleo on a Budget*, dedicated to the budget side of the Paleo lifestyle. She, along with her husband, dog, and cat, reside in Concord, NH, where they can be found photographing weddings for fun and building websites. You can learn more about her and her blog at www.Paleoonabudget.com.